DATE DUE

Volume III
The Great Depression and World War II
(1930–1945)

The Twentieth Century

The Progressive Era and
the First World War
(1900–1918)

The Roaring Twenties and
an Unsettled Peace
(1919–1929)

The Great Depression
and World War II
(1930–1945)

Postwar Prosperity
and the Cold War
(1946–1963)

The Civil Rights Movement
and the Vietnam Era
(1964–1975)

Baby Boomers and the
New Conservatism
(1976–1991)

Volume III
The Great Depression and World War II
(1930–1945)

Editorial Consultants

Matthew T. Downey, University of California at Berkeley

Harvey Green, Northeastern University

David M. Katzman, University of Kansas

Ruth Jacknow Markowitz, SUNY College at Oswego

Albert E. Moyer, Virginia Polytechnic Institute

Macmillan Publishing Company

New York

Maxwell Macmillan Canada

Toronto

...............by Visual Education Corporation,
Princeton, N.J.

Project Editor: Richard Bohlander

Associate Project Editor: Michael Gee

Writers: Linda Barrett, Cathie Cush, Galen Guengerich,
Lois Markham, Donna Singer

Editors: Risa Cottler, Susan Garver, Amy Lewis, Linda Scher,
Betty Shanley, Bonnie Swaim, Frances Wiser

Production Supervisor: Mary Lyn Sodano

Inputting: Cindy Feldner

Interior Design: Maxson Crandall

Cover Design: Mike McIver

Layout: Maxson Crandall, Lisa Evans, Graphic Typesetting
Service, Elizabeth Onorato

Photo Research: Cynthia Cappa, Sara Matthews

Maps: Parrot Graphics

Graphs: Virtual Media

Proofreading Management: Amy Davis

Grateful acknowledgment is made for permission to reprint
the following previously published material:

"Flat Foot Floogee" by Slim Gaillard, Slam Stewart,
and Bud Green. Copyright 1938 (renewed) by Jewel
Music Publishing Co., Inc.
All rights reserved
Reprinted by permission

Photo Credits

AP/Wide World Photos: 3 (3rd, 4th from left), 60, 65, 76, 112

Brown Brothers: 72, 102, 108

Courtesy of General Dynamics Corporation: 31

Culver Pictures, Inc.: 3 (far left), 10

Franklin D. Roosevelt Library: 33

Library of Congress: 3 (2nd from left), 34, 74

National Archives: 53

Photoworld/FPG International: 105

Rockefeller Center, Inc.: 64

The Bettmann Archive: 3 (5th from left), 13, 16 (left), 46, 49, 52, 59, 81,
90, 93, 94, 103, 111

The Library of Congress: 15

UPI/Bettmann: 3 (far right), 14, 16 (right), 18, 23, 25, 36, 39, 44, 50,
79, 82, 83 84, 95, 96, 97, 100, 106, 114, 116, 117

UPI/Bettmann Newsphotos: 12, 26, 40, 58, 66, 70, 71, 86, 88, 89, 101

Visual Education Archives: 55

Macmillan Publishing Company
866 Third Avenue
New York, NY 10022

Maxwell Macmillan Canada, Inc.
1200 Eglinton Avenue East, Suite 200
Don Mills, Ontario M3C 3N1

Macmillan Publishing Company is part of the Maxwell
Communication Group of Companies

Printed in the United States of America

printing number
1 2 3 4 5 6 7 8 9 10

Library of Congress Cataloging-in-Publication Data

The twentieth century / consultants, Matthew T. Downey . . .
[et al.].
    p.   cm.
    Includes index.
    Contents: v. 1. The Progressive Era and the First World War
(1900–1918)—v. 2. The Roaring Twenties and an Unsettled
Peace (1919–1929)—v. 3. The Great Depression and World
War II (1930–1945)—v. 4. Postwar Prosperity and the Cold
War (1946–1963)—v. 5. The Civil Rights Movement and the
Vietnam Era (1964–1975)—v. 6. Baby Boomers and the New
Conservatism (1976–1991).
    ISBN 0-02-897442-5 (set : alk. paper)
    1. History, Modern—20th century. I. Downey, Matthew T.
D421.T88 1992
909.82—dc20   91-40862

Preface

The Twentieth Century is a six-book series covering the major developments of the period, from a primarily American perspective. This is the chronicle of a century unlike any before, one in which the pace of change has accelerated to the point that it is almost overwhelming.

As the century draws to a close, with such major ongoing events as the end of the Cold War and the seeming collapse of communism, it is appropriate to step back from the furious rush forward and examine the significance of the many changes we have seen in what may be the most momentous epoch in the history of the world.

Here, then, is the story of a world transformed by technology: by radio, television, and satellite communications; by automobiles, airplanes, and space travel; by antibiotics, organ transplants, and genetic engineering; by the atomic bomb; by the computer. These are just a few of the advances that have revolutionized the workings of the world and our daily lives.

Here also is the story of a century of history strongly influenced by individuals: Vladimir Lenin and Mao Ze-dong; Franklin Delano Roosevelt, Winston Churchill, and Adolf Hitler; Lech Walesa and Mikhail Gorbachev; Mohandas Gandhi and Martin Luther King Jr.; Theodore Roosevelt, John F. Kennedy, and Ronald Reagan. All have been featured actors in the drama of our times, as conveyed by these pages.

Above all else, it is the story of an American century, one in which a young democratic nation emerged as the world's most powerful force. Through two bitter world wars and an enduring cold war, the dominant influence of the United States on twentieth-century world history and culture is undeniable.

It is the story of the many forces that have transformed the face of our nation from a primarily rural, agricultural society dominated by white people of European heritage to a modern urban, industrialized, and multicultural nation. It is a story of the challenges, successes, and failures that have accompanied these fundamental changes.

Each book of this series focuses on a distinct era of the century. The six titles in the series are:

*The Progressive Era and
    the First World War (1900–1918)*

*The Roaring Twenties and
    an Unsettled Peace (1919–1929)*

*The Great Depression
    and World War II (1930–1945)*

*Postwar Prosperity
    and the Cold War (1946–1963)*

*The Civil Rights Movement
    and the Vietnam Era (1964–1975)*

*Baby Boomers and the
    New Conservatism (1976–1991)*

Each book is divided into six units: The Nation, The World, Business and Economy, Science and Technology, Arts and Entertainment, and Sports and Leisure. The second page of each unit includes a Datafile presenting significant statistical information in both table and graph format. All units include boxed features and sidebars focusing on particular topics of interest.

Additional features of each book include a graphic timeline of events of the period called Glimpses of the Era; a compilation of quotes, headlines, slogans, and literary extracts called Voices of the Era; a glossary of terms; a list of suggested readings; and a complete index.

The series is illustrated with historical photos, as well as original maps, graphs, and tables conveying pertinent statistical data.

Contents

1930

Feb. 18 Pluto discovered by C. W. Tombaugh

May 4 Robert Frost wins Pulitzer Prize for *Collected Poems*

Sept. 15 Comic strip *Blondie* introduced

Nov. 17 Bobby Jones completes "Grand Slam" of golf

1931

Mar. 3 "Star-Spangled Banner" officially becomes U.S. national anthem

Sept. 18 Japan invades Manchuria

Oct. 17 Al Capone sentenced to prison for tax fraud

Nov. 13 Whitney Museum of American Art opens in New York City

1932

Jan. 12 Justice Oliver Wendell Holmes Jr. retires from Supreme Court

Mar. 6 "March King" John Philip Sousa dies

May 21 Pilot Amelia Earhart is first woman to fly solo across Atlantic

Dec. 27 Radio City Music Hall, world's largest theater, opens in New York City

1933

Jan. 30 Adolf Hitler takes office as chancellor of Germany

Mar. 4 Franklin D. Roosevelt becomes 32nd president

Nov. 16 U.S. extends formal diplomatic recognition of Soviet Union

Dec. 17 Chicago Bears beat New York Giants 23–21 in first NFL championship game

1934

Apr. 18 First laundromat opens

Aug. 6 U.S. Marines pull out of Haiti after 19-year occupation

Aug. 15 William Beebe and Otis Barton navigate bathysphere a record 3,028 feet below sea level

Nov. 21 Cole Porter's musical *Anything Goes* opens

1935

May 6 Works Progress Administration established

May 24 First night baseball game played in Cincinnati

June 10 Alcoholics Anonymous founded

Oct. 2 Italy invades Ethiopia

1936

Mar. 7 Germany seizes Rhineland

Aug. 16 At Berlin Olympic Games, Jesse Owens wins 4 gold medals in track and field

Nov. 23 *Life* magazine begins publication

Dec. 10 Edward VIII abdicates throne to marry Wallis Simpson

1937

May 27 Golden Gate Bridge opens in San Francisco

June 22 Joe Louis wins world heavyweight boxing title

July 18 U.S. Navy ends 16-day search for Amelia Earhart

Sept. 26 Blues singer Bessie Smith killed in auto accident

GLIMPSES OF THE ERA

Mar. 12	Germany takes control of Austria
June 25	Minimum wage law (Fair Labor Standards Act) passed
Oct. 30	Orson Welles and Mercury Theatre broadcast *War of the Worlds*
Nov. 9–10	*Kristallnacht*—widespread violence against Jews breaks out across Germany

1938

1939

Apr. 9	Opera star Marian Anderson gives outdoor concert at Lincoln Memorial
July 4	Lou Gehrig retires from baseball
Aug. 4	Francisco Franco becomes Spanish head of state
Sept. 1	Nazi Germany invades Poland. World War II begins in Europe

Feb. 29	Hattie McDaniel becomes first African-American to win an Oscar (Best Supporting Actress in *Gone with the Wind*)
May 10	British prime minister Neville Chamberlain steps down. Winston Churchill takes over
July 27	Bugs Bunny first appears in *A Wild Hare*
Nov. 5	Franklin D. Roosevelt becomes first president to be elected to a third term

1940

1941

Mar. 17	National Gallery of Art opens in Washington, D.C.
June 22	Germany invades Soviet Union
Oct. 9	President Roosevelt gives go-ahead to Manhattan Project
Nov. 1	Mount Rushmore Memorial opens in South Dakota
Dec. 7	Japan attacks U.S. naval base at Pearl Harbor
Dec. 8	U.S. enters World War II

Feb. 19	Internment of Japanese-Americans authorized by Executive Order 9066
May 29	"White Christmas," the biggest-selling record of all time, recorded by Bing Crosby
June 4–7	Allies halt Japanese advance in Battle of Midway
Nov. 28	Fire at Coconut Grove nightclub in Boston kills 487 people

1942

1943

Mar. 31	Rodgers and Hammerstein's *Oklahoma!* opens
Apr. 13	President Roosevelt dedicates Jefferson Memorial
June 20–22	Race riots in Detroit leave 35 dead and over 700 injured
Sept. 9	Allied forces invade Italy

June 6	Invasion of Normandy by Allied forces
July 12	Coca-Cola Company manufactures its one-billionth gallon of cola syrup in Atlanta, Georgia
Aug. 25	Allied forces liberate Paris
Dec. 24	Band leader Glenn Miller officially declared lost at sea

1944

1945

Apr. 12	FDR dies. Truman becomes 33rd president
May 7	Berlin falls to Allies. Germany surrenders
Aug. 6, 9	U.S. drops atomic bombs on Hiroshima and Nagasaki
Sept. 2	Japan formally surrenders, ending World War II
Oct. 24	United Nations established

THE NATION

As the battleship Arizona burned (above), the United States was jolted by another trauma. Japan's attack on Pearl Harbor plunged the nation into World War II. Once the shock passed, Americans rolled up their sleeves to help. United against a common enemy, people worked and fought together. The war brought death and suffering. It also ushered in a period of economic growth that finally removed all traces of the Depression, the nightmare that had lasted 12 years.

The economic growth, personal optimism, and high standard of living of the 1920s had collapsed beginning in 1929. These were replaced by the hallmarks of the Great Depression—economic failure, despair, and uncertainty. Somber times challenged the American

AT A GLANCE

► **Hoover and the Depression**

► **Hard Times**

► **The Election of 1932**

► **Roosevelt's New Deal**

► **The Impact of the New Deal**

► **The Shadow of War**

► **Uncle Sam Goes to War**

people's will to endure. No such economic crisis had ever before tested the federal government.

The Hoover administration had assured Americans that "prosperity is just around the corner." Yet the nation's struggle for economic well-being steadily lost ground. Hope rose, however, after Franklin Delano Roosevelt entered the White House in 1933. Roosevelt's programs, known together as the "New Deal," breathed new life into the economy and lifted people's spirits. The sheer number of New Deal laws plus Roosevelt's leadership not only softened the Depression but also set American politics on a new course. That course featured a strengthened federal government, expanded power for the president, and the beginnings of a modern welfare state.

DATAFILE

U.S. population	1930	1940	1950
Total (in millions)	122.8	131.7	150.7
Urban	56.2%	56.5%	64.0%
Rural	43.8%	43.5%	36.0%
White	89.8%	89.7%	89.5%
Black	9.7%	9.8%	10.0%
Other	0.5%	0.5%	0.5%

Social data	1930	1945
Birthrate (live births per 1,000 pop.)	21.3	20.4
Mortality rate (per 1,000 pop.)	11.3	10.6
Murder rate (per 100,000 pop.)......	8.8	5.7
Persons ages 5–17 in school (per 100 pop.)	89.5	90.5

Voter turnout			
1932 .... 56.9%		1940 .... 62.5%
1936 .... 61.0%		1944 .... 55.9%

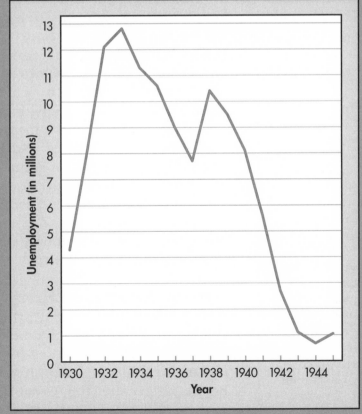

OUT OF WORK
The Rise and Fall of Unemployment, 1930–1945

Source: Stanley Lebergott, *Manpower in Economic Growth: The American Record Since 1800*, table A-3. (Copyright 1964; used with permission of McGraw-Hill Book Company, New York.)

HOOVER AND THE DEPRESSION

Herbert Hoover began his presidency in 1929 on a wave of public optimism and a belief in continued prosperity. He left office on March 4, 1933, in the middle of the worst depression the nation has ever seen. By that date about 15 million people were jobless, the country's banking system had collapsed, and the federal government's limited attempts to rescue the economy had failed.

When the stock market crash of 1929 brought fear for the future, Hoover and other leaders believed the crisis would not last long. They remained optimistic and took no immediate action. The president was a strong supporter of individualism and **private enterprise.** He opposed any measures that would give government food or money directly to needy people. Such action was considered a dole, or handout, and ran against his ideal of self-reliance.

Hoover's initial position on the Depression was that "economic depression cannot be cured by legislative action or executive pronouncement." In his December 3, 1929, State of the Union speech, the president assured the country that the economy would heal itself.

Hoover Takes Steps

The crash hit the rich first, but by 1930 the Depression had affected all members of society. Political leaders recognized the spread of suffering and poverty but publicly preached optimism. Hoover tried to convince people that "what the country needs is a good big laugh." Dead set against federal assistance, the president asked businesses to cooperate with state and local agencies that were trying to help the growing number of hungry, jobless, and homeless people. But these voluntary programs could not meet the needs of all those seeking relief, especially by 1932. Hoover even brought business leaders to Washington for a series of conferences. His aim was to persuade them to maintain current levels of investment and employment. An unprecedented use of presidential authority, these actions had little effect.

By 1930 Hoover had changed his thinking on the causes of the Depression. He now felt that cheap imported European farm products had driven down farm prices and ruined American farmers. As a result, Congress passed the Hawley-Smoot Tariff bill, which imposed import **tariffs** on foreign goods. The measure was supposed to help American farmers compete. In reality, however, it did not help.

As the Depression worsened, people lost confidence in Hoover. The Democrat-controlled Congress demanded a large-scale federal relief effort. Finally, by the end of 1931 the president was forced to take more direct action. First, he introduced a one-year moratorium, or delay, on debt payments that European countries owed the United States for World War I. This slightly eased the economic situation abroad.

Next, he formed the Reconstruction Finance Corporation, which had the authority to issue tax-exempt bonds and to extend credit. It was hoped that loans to banks and businesses would promote economic growth, which would eventually help individuals. The scope and functions of the corporation were extended in July 1932. However, by the November 1932 presidential election, the agency had lent only 10 percent of the money available to it. The situation was desperate, but only cautious steps were being taken.

Hoover Takes the Blame

Prior to the 1929 crash, Herbert Hoover had stood as a symbol of the "American Dream." A self-made millionaire and a man of principle, he was often called the "Great Humanitarian." His election to the presidency inspired people to feel that they had an efficient businessman to run the country.

Hauptmann Convicted in Lindbergh Baby Kidnapping

On March 1, 1932, an intruder took 20-month-old Charles A. Lindbergh Jr. from his crib and killed him. A note left in the baby's nursery assured the parents that their son was safe and instructed them to pay a ransom of $50,000 in small bills.

It was a crushing blow not only to the parents, Colonel Charles A. Lindbergh and Anne Morrow Lindbergh, but to the whole nation. Americans revered Colonel Lindbergh for making the first solo transatlantic flight, in 1927. In September 1934 a tip from a gas station attendant led to the arrest of Bruno Hauptmann. Hauptmann's trial, conducted amidst furious press coverage, lasted for six lurid weeks. He was convicted of first-degree murder on Valentine's Day 1935 and was electrocuted less than two months later. The question of his guilt is argued to this day.

As the crisis continued, this perception changed. Hoover was accused of using the federal government to help the nation's banks and businesses while refusing to help the millions of unemployed and starving. The people lost confidence in his leadership, and he became an object of ridicule, his name often being used in connection with the visible signs of the Depression. "Hoover blankets" were the old newspapers the homeless slept under at night; "Hoover flags" were the empty pocket linings of the unemployed, turned inside out. The hundreds of shantytowns that sprang up on the outskirts of cities, where the homeless made crude shelters from cardboard, newspaper, and metal scraps, were mockingly called "Hoovervilles." Hoover's own campaign slogan—"a chicken in every pot"—came back to haunt him. His 1928 campaign had proclaimed how well off people would be under the probusiness Republicans. The hungry jobless during the Depression used the phrase mockingly.

Hoover's Legacy

Hoover's efforts to let private business recover on its own and to use volunteerism as the means for ending individual hardship did not work. Their failure, however, made the country more willing to accept Roosevelt's New Deal policy of federal intervention in the economy. Hoover's Reconstruction Finance Corporation was really a forerunner of many New Deal programs. However, it was up to Roosevelt—and the war—to pull the country out of the Great Depression.

▲ Seattle's Hooverville, shown here, was just like the shantytown of every other city. The poor and jobless, thrown out of their homes or apartments, built crude shacks on the fringes of the city.

HARD TIMES

Men selling apples on street corners, families wandering across the country looking for jobs, long lines of people waiting outside soup kitchens for a crust of bread or a bowl of thin soup—these were the scenes of the Great Depression. During the 1930s, poverty became a way of life for 40 million Americans. When the federal government failed to provide any help, private organizations and charities gave relief. At first many people were ashamed to seek handouts, but desperation finally drove them to these agencies' doors. By 1932, however, many of the agencies were themselves bankrupt and forced to close.

As many as 13 million people, a quarter of the workforce, were unemployed in 1933, one of the Depression's worst years. Without paychecks, many families lost their homes and were forced to

"We are the first nation in the history of the world to go to the poorhouse in an automobile."

—Will Rogers, 1930

The Depression era disrupted almost every aspect of life in the United States. Some of the worst victims of the economic crisis of the thirties were children. Besides not having proper clothing, shelter, or food, many children and young adults were denied an education.

In the fall of 1933 alone, 2,000 rural schools failed to open. More than 1,500 commercial schools and colleges were forced to suspend classes. At least 200,000 certified teachers were left jobless across the country, and an estimated 2,280,000 children did not attend school.

▼ Some states distributed surplus food—fruits, vegetables, flour—to the needy. But as the labels on these bags of flour show, it was forbidden to sell these relief packages.

build makeshift shelters in vacant lots. One collection of these shacks was in Central Park in New York City; another was near the White House in Washington, D.C. Children from such shantytowns roamed in search of wood and coal for fires and for newspapers to use as blankets. Hungry people rummaged through garbage cans for scraps of food. One person in Chicago reported seeing a crowd of 50 men fighting over a barrel of garbage.

The lack of food and warm clothing led to much illness during cold winters. Families sacrificed medical and dental care, and even cleanliness, because they had to use their money to buy food. Men suffered emotionally from losing their traditional role as breadwinner. Many deserted their families in despair. Children grew up fast because they had to hunt for work as soon as they were old enough to help. The memories of one Chicago woman vividly describe the hardships:

My father lost his job and we moved into a double-garage. The landlord didn't charge us rent for seven years. We had a coal stove, and we had to each take turns, the three of us kids, to warm our legs. . . .

He [my father] always could get something to feed us kids. We lived about three months on candy cods, they're little chocolate square things. We had these melted in milk. And he had a part-time job in a Chinese restaurant. We lived on those fried noodles. I can't stand 'em today. [Terkel, *Hard Times*, p. 116]

A series of natural disasters during the 1930s—especially droughts and dust storms on the Great Plains—increased the suffering of the country's farmers. Many of them lost their farms and became migrant workers, trying to stay alive as they traveled across the country to harvest crops for very little money.

Farmers were not the only sufferers, though. For the first time in history, many white-collar workers, such as doctors, lawyers, and engineers, were out of work and standing in breadlines. A few people committed suicide, especially right after the crash. But most Americans tried to hang on and even managed to keep a sense of humor. One popular joke told of a hotel clerk who asked a guest as he registered, "Do you want the room for sleeping or for jumping?"

Those people lucky enough to keep their jobs during the Depression had their wages reduced. It was during this time that the five-day work week became standard. Business owners adopted a shorter work week so that they would be paying workers for fewer hours.

As unemployment spread, so did labor unrest. Workers staged a

The Dust Bowl: Exodus from the Plains

One of the worst environmental disasters in U.S. history occurred in the 1930s. Its setting was the Great Plains, where western winds picked up loose soil and swirled it into furious dust storms. Dust from these storms spread as far as the Atlantic and Pacific coasts. The land was so severely damaged in parts of New Mexico, Texas, Oklahoma, Kansas, and Colorado that the entire area was called the "Dust Bowl." More than 50 million acres of land became too barren for farming, and another 50 million acres were seriously threatened.

Two situations created the Dust Bowl. First, several generations of farmers and ranchers had plowed up grasslands and cut more and more trees to make room for fields and pastures. This destroyed the root system, which increased erosion. Second, the plains experienced a terrible drought from 1931 to 1938. Crops and grasses for grazing livestock withered and died. Without live roots to hold it down, the dry soil was whipped into dust by strong winds.

People and animals who were caught outdoors during a storm could suffer damage to their lungs (called "dust pneumonia") or die from suffocation. Blowing dust got into food, spoiling its taste. It ruined cars and farm machinery. After a storm, people had to shovel dirt out of their homes and try to replant their crops.

Thousands of Dust Bowl farmers went bankrupt and were forced to sell personal belongings at auction or to junk dealers. Many ruined farm families took to the road in search of a better life. Large numbers headed toward California, where there was a promise of work in the fields. They left in old, worn-out vehicles or on foot, taking with them what few possessions they still had. Any livestock that was left, such as chickens or pigs, was killed and salted down for food on the journey.

Many who reached California were turned away by state police. Those who got through found only more hardship and suffering. When they could find work—picking a seasonal crop—the pay was very poor. Many families lived in hovels and had little hope for anything better.

In order to stop the destruction from the dust storms and help the farmers, the federal government established the Soil Conservation Service in 1935. This agency taught farmers how to protect the soil and slow the erosion process. It also planted trees in certain areas of the Great Plains to break the force of the winds. This step was called the Shelterbelt Project. These and other measures have so far warded off any repetition of the Dust Bowl.

Gangsters at Large: Robin Hoods or Hoodlums?

Bonnie (left) and Clyde were just two of the many vicious gangsters who robbed and murdered during the Depression. The 1930s crime wave was unlike the bootleg-based organized gangsterism of the 1920s.

———

While millions of jobless Americans stood in breadlines, certain lawbreakers toting tommy guns and sawed-off shotguns crisscrossed rural America, robbing banks and shooting it out with the police. The rampages of John Dillinger, Bonnie and Clyde, Machine Gun Kelly, Pretty Boy Floyd, and Ma Barker and her boys were familiar stories in every household. These criminals were not part of any organized crime family. They worked alone or with a few followers, escaping the law in fast cars. Some enjoyed heroic images among Americans who had lost everything in the Depression.

John Dillinger became the most widely known bank robber of the time. He held up banks in six states, killed ten men, and escaped twice after being captured. FBI director J. Edgar Hoover had a 40-member squad devoted exclusively to capturing Dillinger. The hoodlum managed to outwit both federal and local authorities until he was killed in 1934 by federal agents outside the Biograph Theatre in Chicago. He had been betrayed by the mysterious "Lady in Red." Many Americans pictured Dillinger as a Robin Hood figure who robbed the rich. The public gave him the nickname "Gentleman Johnny" because of his manners and well-dressed look.

The gallery of gangsters from the 1930s crime wave contains many other colorful but vicious people. George "Machine Gun" Kelly, who was a bank robber and murderer, claimed he could write his name with bullets on a barn door. Charles "Pretty Boy" Floyd robbed more than 30 midwestern banks during a 12-year period before being captured. He was known for his good looks and his habit of carving a notch on his pocket watch each time he killed a man.

Arizonan Kate "Ma" Barker involved her four sons in a crime spree of robbery and murder—yet made them go to church on Sunday. Finally, there was the Barrow gang, composed of Bonnie Parker, Clyde Barrow, and their followers. Although the Hollywood film *Bonnie and Clyde* glamorized these people, they were merciless killers and bank robbers. Police from five states pursued them from 1932 until they were killed in 1934.

These 1930s gangsters had one long-term effect. Hoover's FBI made a big name for itself—and for Director Hoover—by tracking these criminals down. Hoover stayed in office until the 1970s. He could not be removed in part because of the FBI's enhanced image.

number of protests demanding relief. The jobless banded together in organized action for jobs. In March 1932, some 3,000 unemployed auto workers marched on the Ford plant in Dearborn, Michigan, to demand jobs. Four men were killed and many more wounded during the demonstration.

THE ELECTION OF 1932

Both Democrats and Republicans held their party conventions to choose presidential candidates in the summer of 1932. By this time, the Depression was growing worse almost daily. Most Americans were blaming President Hoover or wealthy businessmen for the continuing crisis. They saw many rich people avoiding taxes and ignoring the suffering of the hard pressed. Most average Americans were tired of waiting; they wanted results! The Republicans nominated Hoover to run for a second term, but few party members expected him to win.

The Democrats could smell victory. They were convinced that the man who won their nomination would carry the party banner into the White House for the first time in over a decade. Some party members backed former New York governor Alfred K. Smith. Others wanted House Speaker John Nance Garner as the candidate. After a spirited convention battle, however, the nomination was won by New York governor Franklin

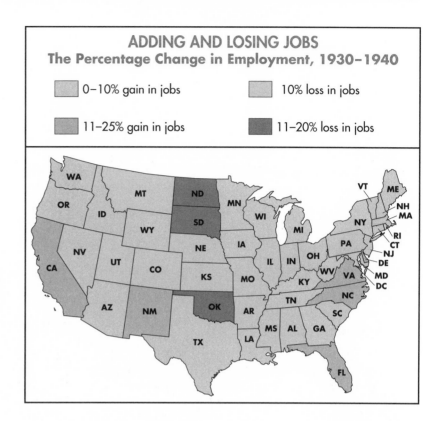

ADDING AND LOSING JOBS
The Percentage Change in Employment, 1930–1940

- 0–10% gain in jobs
- 11–25% gain in jobs
- 10% loss in jobs
- 11–20% loss in jobs

Delano Roosevelt. He was seen by many as a heroic figure in the tradition of his cousin, former president Theodore Roosevelt.

FDR: The Man and the Moment

A member of a well-known family, FDR had dedicated his life to public service. Before he became governor of New York, he served as a New York state senator from 1910 to 1913. Later, he distinguished himself as assistant secretary of the Navy during the presidency of Woodrow Wilson (1913–1920). In that post, he had spoken in favor of a big Navy, a strong presidency, and a policy of preparedness. The Democratic convention in 1920 had chosen Roosevelt as its vice presidential candidate. The Democrats had lost the 1920 election, but Roosevelt had won national exposure.

▲ This map of job growth for each state throughout the 1930s shows the harsh effect of the Dust Bowl. The states with the greatest overall loss of jobs are Oklahoma, North Dakota, and South Dakota. Kansas and Nebraska had nearly a 10 percent job loss, too. Note the high job growth in California, Florida, and Washington, D.C.

While governor of New York (1928–1932), Roosevelt introduced several progressive programs. He reformed the civil service and started such **social welfare programs** as state-supported old-age pensions and unemployment insurance (a system of temporary government pay for laid-off workers). He also became the first governor in the country to set up a relief agency when the Depression worsened in 1931.

Two events in Roosevelt's personal life had a tremendous impact on his public life. The first was his marriage to Eleanor Roosevelt, a distant cousin of his and

"Rendezvous with Destiny": The Roosevelt Style

Franklin Delano Roosevelt was a man of great charm and an iron will. As a leader, he inspired confidence in the American people. In his first inaugural address, he challenged the nation to face up to its problems, saying, "the only thing we have to fear is fear itself—nameless, unreasoning, unjustified terror which paralyzes needed efforts to convert retreat into advance." He set the tone for his presidency when he further stated, "This Nation asks for action, and action now."

Indeed, he took action that was swift and decisive. He listened to the new ideas of the brilliant people whom he gathered around him, then made quick decisions. He was flexible as well as practical, insisting: "Take a method and try it. If it fails, try another. But above all, try something."

Among the many successes of Roosevelt's presidential style were his frequent radio talks, called

"fireside chats." FDR's informal, reassuring tones personalized his relationship with the American people. Often beginning with the expression "My friends," Roosevelt went on to explain his programs and to win support for them. Radio addresses became the most effective way to reach the American people that any president had yet used.

A warm smile, a sense of humor, and a clenched cigarette holder were Roosevelt's trademarks. He expertly drew public attention away from his physical handicap and personally looked beyond the limitations it imposed. The press helped by never showing him in a wheelchair. His wife, Eleanor, became "his eyes and his ears." She attended many public functions as his representative and even visited troops overseas on his behalf during World War II. A keen observer, Eleanor kept her husband well informed; he valued her opinions immensely.

Roosevelt the private man enjoyed sailing, fishing, and collecting stamps and books. Swimming and visits to the medicinal waters in Warm Springs, Georgia, helped relieve tensions from his paralysis and his hectic schedule. He even formed the Warm Springs Foundation to help other polio victims.

In the final analysis, Roosevelt's style of leadership stood out because he had the common touch. He spoke to the American people personally, directly, in plain English, and made them feel that he was just another one of them.

a niece of Teddy Roosevelt. Eleanor was an independent, tough-minded woman who supported her husband's ideas and focused attention on problems of the underprivileged, women, and racial minorities. The second major influence was Roosevelt's bout with polio, which struck him in 1921 and left both legs paralyzed. With Eleanor's help, he rose above the emotional and physical effects of this handicap and became even more determined to pursue his political career.

FDR: Campaign for Victory

Before the 1932 political convention, Roosevelt had assembled a group of Columbia University professors to help him outline a series of programs that might combat the Depression. These men, often called the "Brain Trust," sketched out ideas, some of which would become the New Deal. At the convention, Roosevelt was prepared with a confident approach to solving the nation's problems. He promised America a New Deal; the Democrats gave him the nomination.

While Hoover campaigned on the theory that private business would rescue the country, Roosevelt declared that personal incomes needed to be more equal. He further stated that the basic causes of the Depression were the problems of the farmers and their inability to buy goods. In an early radio address Roosevelt set the tone for his campaign. He said the country needed plans "that build from the bottom up and not from the top down; that put . . . faith once more in the forgotten man at the bottom of the economic pyra-

mid." He promised a program of social change and federal support for the economy. He pledged the federal government to immediate relief efforts, conservation, public works spending, and social insurance. His main promise was that the government would act. Roosevelt promised to try something.

An incident during the summer of 1932 almost ensured a Roosevelt victory. Twenty thousand jobless veterans gathered in Washington to demand immediate payment of a bonus that they were due to receive in 1945. Although the protest was orderly, Hoover called on the Army to break it up. The image of tanks, bayonets, and tear gas used against hungry, unemployed men who had fought for their country dismayed many Americans. In the November election, Roosevelt won all but six states. The Democrats also retained control of Congress. The stage was set for Roosevelt to start his New Deal.

ROOSEVELT'S NEW DEAL

The rains had stopped and dry weather was forecast for Washington, D.C., on March 4, 1933. By about mid-morning, Franklin Delano Roosevelt was raising his hand and taking the presidential oath of office. Many Americans viewed the clearing skies as an omen of better times ahead for the whole country. The result was less promising. Only with the U.S. entry into World War II did the

Depression end. Yet Americans continued to place faith in FDR. By the end of his life, he had been elected to the presidency four times. He forged a new Democratic coalition that broke the Republican hold on the White House. He also continued the century's trend toward a larger, more powerful federal government—and a more powerful presidency.

The new president used his inaugural address to stress the need for cooperation, compassion, and social values over material gain. He declared, "We now realize as we have never realized before our interdependence on each other; that we cannot merely take, but must give as well." He compared the Depression to war and summoned Americans to join the fight. He tried to combat despair with a call to action.

Pledging immediate action, Roosevelt took steps the first Monday after his inauguration. First, he suspended most operations of the nation's banks in a four-day "bank holiday." This step prevented depositors, who were panicking, from withdrawing any more funds. Next, he called a special session of Congress and persuaded legislators to pass his Emergency Banking Act. Then he spoke directly to the people over the radio in his first "fireside chat." His words explained banking in terms everyone could understand. When the banks reopened, they had more deposits than withdrawals. The banking crisis was over.

The nation was revived. As Arthur Krock wrote in his March 12, 1933, *New York Times* column, "Never was there such a change in the transfer of a government. The President is the boss, the dynamo, the works!"

The First New Deal

Roosevelt kept Congress in special session for 100 days and pushed through 15 new laws that radically changed the relationship between the American people and the federal government. His two goals during these "first hundred days"— sometimes called the "First New Deal"—were to bring relief to suffering Americans and to promote recovery. At Roosevelt's urging, Congress created several agencies to carry out the New Deal's first laws. They became called the "al-

Major Acts of the New Deal

Emergency Banking Act	1933	Permitted government inspectors to check banks' records and to reopen only financially stable banks
Truth-in-Securities Act	1933	Required firms to give investors financial information
Glass-Steagall Banking Act	1933	Created the Federal Deposit Insurance Corporation to protect bank depositors
National Industrial Recovery Act	1933	Founded the National Recovery Administration, which enforced fair practice codes for business and industry, including minimum wages, maximum hours, and quality and production standards. Declared unconstitutional by Supreme Court in 1935
National Labor Relations Act	1935	Protected the rights of workers by allowing them to form unions
Social Security Act	1935	Provided funds for the aged, the jobless, the blind and disabled, and needy children
U.S. Housing Act	1937	Provided money for federal public housing programs
Fair Labor Standards Act	1938	Protected workers by setting minimum wage and limiting the workweek to 44 hours; set minimum age for factory workers at 16

phabet agencies" because most people knew them by their initials rather than their full names.

The National Recovery Administration (NRA) was created as a means for businesses to regulate such things as prices, wages, and working conditions to ensure fair competition. Although business leaders criticized the NRA, it helped the economy recover until it was declared unconstitutional by the Supreme Court in 1935. A more lasting agency was the Public Works Administration (PWA). The PWA put many of the unemployed back to work and encouraged recovery by creating jobs on federally funded construction projects across the country. The Lincoln Tunnel between New Jersey and Manhattan is an example.

Creation of the Civilian Conservation Corps (CCC) provided jobs for young unmarried urban men in a variety of conservation projects, such as tree planting and drought relief. By 1935 the number of men working in 2,600 CCC camps totaled 500,000. By 1942 about 3 million men aged 17 to 25, including 9,000 Native Americans, could claim to have worked at one time or another for the CCC.

The most important New Deal work-relief agency was the Works Progress Administration (WPA). It provided more than 8 million jobs and funded the construction of hundreds of thousands of public buildings and facilities between 1935 and 1941. WPA workers built scores of projects, including LaGuardia Airport in New York City and the 470-mile Blue Ridge Parkway. That road connects Shenandoah National Park in Vir-

ginia to Great Smokies National Park in Tennessee.

FDR and Congress dealt with the plight of the American farmer through the Agricultural Adjustment Administration (AAA). Many economists believed that one of the basic reasons for the continuing Depression was overproduction. As a result, this agency was designed to pay farmers to reduce production in order to raise prices and increase farm income. The federal government also started credit and loan agencies to bring mortgage relief to farmers and homeowners.

The most far-reaching measures of the first New Deal were the creation of the Federal Deposit Insurance Corporation (FDIC) and the Tennessee Valley Authority (TVA). The FDIC protects people from losing their money by insuring bank deposits up to a certain amount. This protection of depositors has since become one of the cornerstones of personal financial security for Americans.

By creating the TVA, Roosevelt and Congress took a bold step. They established the principle that the federal government had the right—and the responsibility—to direct land use and provide public utilities. The seven-state Tennessee River valley had been hard hit by both the Depression and frequent flooding. The TVA set up a government corporation that constructed dams, built hydroelectric power plants, sold cheap electricity, promoted better agricultural practices, and introduced welfare programs among the area's poverty-stricken residents. In most circles, the TVA was hailed as a New Deal success.

21ST AMENDMENT ENDS PROHIBITION

December 5, 1933, marked the end of what most Americans felt was a failed experiment—Prohibition. By the late 1920s, a political struggle between those in favor of repealing Prohibition, the "wets," and those against repeal, the "drys," was in full force. Congress decided that a popular vote was needed; it wanted the people to decide whether Prohibition was necessary.

Special state conventions were held in 1933 to ratify the proposed Twenty-first Amendment that would repeal Prohibition. Finally, on December 5, 1933, Utah cast the thirty-sixth and final vote needed to ratify the Twenty-first Amendment. The Great Experiment was over.

But it did not escape controversy. For the first time in history the federal government had gone into business and competed directly with private companies.

Another major step was the creation of the Securities and Exchange Commission (SEC). Signed into law in 1934, the Securities Exchange Act established the SEC to regulate stock exchange operations. The SEC became a powerful government agency in the following decades.

The Second New Deal

After getting relief and recovery programs off the ground, Roosevelt turned to his third New Deal goal: reform. Thus began the Second New Deal, one of the most significant periods of reform legislation in American history. In 1935 the president chose to champion labor and the underprivileged rather than try to please both business and workers as he had during the First New Deal. Congress passed two laws in that year that have affected every citizen ever since.

The Social Security Act provided government pensions for retired workers, small paychecks for jobless workers, and aid for the handicapped. These payments were funded by a payroll tax paid by workers and employers. The Wagner Act, or National Labor Rela-

Roosevelt and the Supreme Court

Roosevelt's long tenure as president allowed him to appoint eight associate justices to the Supreme Court and one chief justice, Harlan Fiske Stone (1941). The associate justices were Hugo L. Black (1937), Stanley F. Reed (1938), Felix Frankfurter (1939), William O. Douglas (1939), Frank Murphy (1940), James F. Byrnes (1941), Robert H. Jackson (1941), and Wiley B. Rutledge, Jr. (1943).

The Court that Roosevelt inherited declared several of his New Deal programs unconstitutional during his first term (1933–1937). FDR's plan to pack the Court failed, but it turned out to be unnecessary. The "Nine Old Men," as the conservative justices were called, began upholding New Deal laws. By 1941, FDR's appointments had the Court leaning toward change and reform. This "Roosevelt Court" upheld New Deal legislation and thereby confirmed the federal government's right to expand its role in social and economic affairs.

▼ ▼ ▼

FDR appointed eight associate justices and one chief justice to the Supreme Court.

Among the Court's important rulings was the landmark civil rights case of *Smith v. Allwright* (1944). This decision declared that primary elections must be open to all party members regardless of race. The Court did not always rule in favor of civil rights, however. In the case of *Korematsu v. United States* (1944), the Court upheld the wartime imprisonment of Japanese-Americans, a shameful violation of citizens' rights.

Nevertheless, the Roosevelt Court was known overall for its liberal views. Its influence was far reaching. Four of the justices were still on the Court when racial segregation in public schools was declared unconstitutional in the landmark case of *Brown v. Board of Education* in 1954.

tions Act, outlawed unfair management practices in business and guaranteed workers' right to **collective bargaining** with management. To enforce these steps, it established the powerful National Labor Relations Board. Now backed by federal safeguards, labor unions took on new influence—and thousands of new members. The Wagner Act was, in essence, a bill of rights for workers to organize.

The 1936 Election

Congress also passed income tax laws that were more progressive, raising the rates for those with higher incomes. Although the tax increases placed on the wealthy were much less than the president had proposed, they were enough to give Roosevelt the support of most middle- and lower-income Americans. He easily won the 1936 election, defeating Republican candidate Alfred M. Landon. In his second inaugural address, Roosevelt came out firmly on the side of the working poor. "I see one-third of a nation ill-housed, ill-clad, ill-nourished," he said—and then promised to do something about it.

Roosevelt Under Attack

During his second term Roosevelt found it more difficult to push his reform agenda through Congress. Heavy spending on New Deal programs had increased the national debt. Also, public opinion began to split, either for or against him. Most citizens loved him. But prosperous business people and much of the press hated him. Unable even to say his name, his opponents called him "That Man."

"Every man a king!" was the populist slogan of Louisiana politician Huey Long. Long, a Democrat who completely controlled his state's government, began to challenge FDR's popularity with his Share Our Wealth campaign. Local conflicts did him in, however; he was assassinated in 1935.

The major thorn in Roosevelt's side, however, was the Supreme Court, which was declaring parts of his New Deal legislation **unconstitutional**. In a controversial move, the president proposed adding six more justices—all of whom he would appoint, of course. Congress defeated this proposal to "pack the Court," but it did pass a bill guaranteeing justices a pension at age 70. This encouraged some of the older justices to retire and gave Roosevelt the chance to appoint some justices more favorable to the New Deal.

However, the president's attempts to "pack the Court" turned much of Congress against him. He created more tension in 1938, when he tried during Senate elections to oust Democratic senators who were unfriendly to his New Deal. He even used a fireside chat to try to gain voter support for this move. Voters would have none of

One of the strangest get-rich-quick schemes of the 1930s was the "send a dime" chain-letter craze. Here is how it worked: After receiving a chain letter in the mail with six names and addresses at the bottom, you were supposed to send a dime to the person at the top of the list, cross off his or her name, and add your own to the bottom of the list. You then sent the letter to five friends. If no one broke the chain, you were eventually supposed to receive 15,625 dimes, or $1,562.50.

Beginning in March 1935, post offices across the country were flooded with such chain letters; postal service slowed considerably. During one week in Denver 90 extra clerks and letter carriers had to be hired. In Des Moines, Iowa, banks ran out of dimes. The Post Office tried unsuccessfully to end the fad. By mid-June, most people had finally lost interest in the scheme and the volume of mail returned to normal. Of course, most of the people who joined the scheme lost money.

Roosevelt's maneuvering; they sent the conservative Democrats back to Congress.

The New Deal also lost support as a result of the **recession** of 1937–1938. Once the recession took hold, many people questioned the effectiveness of the New Deal.

In the midst of this controversy, one other major piece of New Deal legislation was passed in 1938. The Fair Labor Standards Act set national standards for a minimum wage and a maximum number of hours that employees could work.

By 1939 the gross national product had climbed to $91 billion, which was more than 60 percent higher than that of 1933. Both supporters and detractors of the New Deal applauded that good news. The country's economy had still not completely recovered, however. Unemployment stood at 17 percent in 1939.

THE IMPACT OF THE NEW DEAL

Roosevelt's "great experiment," the New Deal, thoroughly changed the relationship between citizen and government. The federal government became bigger and more centralized by taking on authority that it had never had or used before. Much New Deal legislation was based on the principle that government is responsible for the health, welfare, and financial security of its citizens as well as for their freedom and protection. This became the guiding principle of laws for

years to come. Thus, New Deal policies led to the creation in the United States of what is called a **welfare state.** This approach to government has grown and caused controversy ever since.

Changes for the Future

Prior to the New Deal, economic depressions had occurred in fairly regular 15- to 20-year cycles. New Deal programs put in place a protective system to help prevent future recessions from becoming as severe as the Depression of the 1930s. These programs made the **capitalist** economy more responsive to public needs and so helped preserve it. Big business became even bigger, but the federal government imposed certain controls and regulations upon businesses to protect workers and encourage fair competition.

One of the most important results of the New Deal was the promotion of conservation and rehabilitation of the land. As Roosevelt, a dedicated conservationist, said in 1935, "The forests are the 'lungs' of our land, purifying our air and giving fresh strength to our people." His programs stopped the careless destruction of natural resources, restored damaged lands to good agricultural condition, planted trees, and created dams. Other steps expanded the use of water power through such projects as the TVA and the Columbia River project. Roosevelt brought more forest land under federal protection than any president before him. He expanded the number of national parks by opening such places as Washington State's Olympic National Park for all

Americans to enjoy. This careful attention to preserving, protecting, and improving the nation's natural resources laid a firm foundation for the environmental movement of the 1970s and 1980s.

The individual and expanding democratic ideals took center stage during the Roosevelt years. New Deal policies increased social equality by enhancing the average American's security. Before creation of the national minimum wage and Social Security for retired workers, most working Americans were at the mercy of employers and the economic cycles. For the first time federal programs gave many Americans easier access to health care, housing, and jobs. Workers fought to organize unions to represent them. Although much violence was associated with the labor movement in the late 1930s, labor unions began to grow. In later decades they became a powerful force in business and politics.

Many New Deal projects laid the groundwork for future federal programs. For example, President Lyndon Johnson's Head Start program of the 1960s had its origin in the WPA nursery schools project. Adult-education programs of the 1970s and 1980s can be traced to a WPA project that taught thousands of illiterate adults to read.

New Roles for Women and Minorities

During the Depression, as before, women were often discriminated against in employment. Many Americans believed that women who worked for wages were taking jobs that should go to men, the traditional breadwinners. Neverthe-

less, the number of women in the work force increased throughout the 1930s. Quite simply, more women found it necessary to work in order to keep their families going. Also, staffing the new government agencies created many jobs that became identified as "women's work," such as typing and clerical tasks.

Women also gained greater political influence during the New Deal. Frances Perkins became the first woman Cabinet member, and more than 100 other women held senior positions during the Roosevelt presidency.

It was Eleanor Roosevelt, however, who emerged as the best-known and most influential woman of the era. Before her husband became president, Eleanor Roosevelt was active in the League of Women Voters and the Women's Trade Union League. As First Lady she established many "firsts," such as holding weekly press conferences

◄ Eleanor Roosevelt, shown here visiting with coal miners, was a popular and effective First Lady. By reaching such sites, which her polio-stricken husband could not do, she helped get FDR's message to the people—and their messages to him.

with women reporters. She had her own radio program and a syndicated newspaper column called "My Day." She also was a major voice in promoting aid for racial minorities and the underprivileged.

In 1928 black Americans had voted for Hoover and the Republicans, as they had since the 1870s. They broke with tradition during the New Deal. By 1940 the majority of blacks voted Democratic for the first time in history. Although Congress legislated little or nothing in the area of civil rights during the 1930s, blacks benefited greatly from New Deal policies. Also, Roosevelt had taken a stand against racial discrimination by 1935. In May of that year he issued an executive order banning exclusion of blacks from WPA projects. By the end of the decade, 15 to 20 percent of WPA workers were black.

On the recommendation of his wife, the president appointed Mary McLeod Bethune, a black woman who had founded Bethune-Cookman College in Florida, as assistant director of the National Youth Administration. Bethune's work in this agency enabled her to upgrade the condition of many blacks. In 1937 Roosevelt appointed William Hastie as the first black federal judge in American history. He also gathered around him a group of black leaders, nicknamed the "Black Cabinet" by the press, to advise him on blacks' economic problems. Perhaps FDR's most long-lasting contribution to the civil rights movement, however, was his Supreme Court appointees. A number of them later became strong advocates of civil rights for blacks.

Native Americans experienced a notable gain when Congress passed the Indian Reorganization Act of 1934. This legislation remains the basis for federal policy on Native American affairs. It ended land allotments and returned surplus land to tribal ownership.

A Changed Concept of the Presidency

Roosevelt is one of the century's dominant figures in American politics. He transformed the role of the government in American life. Beginning with the Progressives, peo-

National Focus on Civil Rights

Nine young black men were arrested in Paint Rock, Alabama, on March 25, 1931. Two white women had reported to police that these nine men had fought with three white men, chasing them away, and then raped the two women.

Medical examiners could find no evidence of an assault, and months later one of the women retracted her accusation. Nevertheless, the nine youths were tried. The court-appointed attorney for the accused men called no witnesses for their defense. They were all convicted, with eight sentenced to death and one given life imprisonment.

The so-called Scottsboro case became a national left-wing cause. Artists, poets, novelists, and playwrights drew attention to the young men's plight. Newspapers took stands on the case. The publicity stirred a riot in Harlem and a march on the capital. After six trials in Alabama state courts and three appeals to the U.S. Supreme Court, five of the men were freed, and four received life sentences. Four were eventually paroled; the fifth escaped from prison to Michigan, where the governor refused to return him. Evidence released in 1966 showed that all nine had been innocent.

ple had called for greater government action in the economy and society. Republicans had resisted the idea. By using the government to provide jobs, relief, and income security, FDR—and the Democrats in Congress—made that government role a reality.

His actions both in the New Deal and during World War II helped create a more powerful executive branch. Other wartime presidents—such as Lincoln and Wilson—had increased executive power as well. FDR was different. The long list of emergency agencies created in the New Deal extended presidential power to domestic politics. The result was a **bureaucracy** that would keep growing and come to plague the federal government in later years.

FDR also created new alignments in American politics. His elections forged a Democratic coalition that would last until the 1970s and 1980s. That coalition linked workers, city dwellers, Southerners, and blacks.

THE SHADOW OF WAR

In 1933 two men, separated by an ocean, appeared at the center of the world stage, each taking over the leadership of his country. Both persuasive speakers, Franklin Delano Roosevelt and Adolf Hitler were complete opposites in personality and beliefs. They would also become enemies whose actions would drastically change the world. While Roosevelt was expanding democracy and bringing the United States out of the Depression, Hitler was turning Germany into a dictatorship bent on foreign conquest. Germany was not alone, however. During this period, Italy, under dictator Benito Mussolini, invaded Ethiopia, and Japan invaded China.

Isolationism in the 1930s

Even though military threats were growing throughout the world in the 1930s, the United States concentrated on healing its internal problems. Therefore, both Presidents Hoover and Roosevelt declined to form any military alliances in Europe. They refused to join the League of Nations or to get drawn into European politics. Public support for this position was overwhelming; **isolationism** was the preferred policy. Within the Western Hemisphere Roosevelt pursued a "Good Neighbor policy," which strengthened ties with South America and Canada and promoted greater security for all the Americas.

Reflecting the mood of the nation and the president's position, Congress passed three Neutrality Acts (1935, 1936, and 1937) aimed at keeping the United States out of foreign wars. The 1937 act specifically banned arms shipments to either side of any conflict between foreign nations.

FDR Shifts Policy

However, by 1937 Roosevelt began shifting his foreign policy stand and proposed a quarantine of nations ruled by fascism. In 1939 Congress revised the Neutrality Acts to allow Britain to buy arms with cash. By April 1940 Hitler

AMERICA FIRST COMMITTEE CALLS FOR ISOLATION FROM WAR

AMERICA FIRST COMMITTEE CALLS FOR ISOLATION FROM WAR

The United States was sharply divided in the 1930s between isolationists, who cautioned against interference in foreign wars, and interventionists, who believed the United States should help the victims of Germany's and Italy's aggression. A major isolationist group was the America First Committee, which formed in the fall of 1940. The committee included many influential Americans. It had the support of the Hearst newspaper chain and other important newspapers. It also enjoyed indirect support from much of the Republican party. Interest in isolationism began to wane, however, as Adolf Hitler's armored tanks swept across Europe. When Japan attacked Pearl Harbor in 1941, few Americans opposed the declaration of war against Japan.

had formed the Rome-Berlin **Axis** with Mussolini, and German armies occupied much of Western Europe and threatened Great Britain. While most Americans remained caught up in national affairs, Roosevelt watched the rising international tensions with growing concern. He asked Congress for $1.8 billion to finance the greatest peacetime military buildup in U.S. history.

Still claiming a neutral position among the world's warring nations, the president nevertheless asked Congress for still more money—this time to send arms to Britain. As he said, "We will extend to the opponents of force the material resources of this nation." In the fall of 1940 Congress passed the Selective Service and Training Act, which established the first peacetime military service draft in U.S.

history. Although Roosevelt continued to promise Americans that "your boys are not going to be sent into any foreign war," a vocal minority labeled him a "warmonger."

A big question on everyone's lips in the summer of 1940 was whether Roosevelt would run for an unprecedented third term. He remained quiet on the issue but let himself be "drafted" at the Democratic convention. In the election that year, "the barefoot boy from Wall Street," Republican Wendell Willkie, was defeated by FDR.

Growing U.S. Involvement

With the reins of government tightly in his grip again, Roosevelt moved swiftly to get more aid for the British. The British stood nearly alone against Germany and had been enduring severe German bombing raids since August 1940. Using the illustration of lending a neighbor whose house is burning a garden hose, the president proposed a program called "Lend-Lease." When passed by Congress in March 1941, Lend-Lease gave the president extraordinary powers to sell, transfer, lend, or lease war materials to nations whose defense he regarded as necessary to U.S. defense. Thus, the country moved from neutrality to active participation in world affairs; it would be the "arsenal of democracy."

Most Americans supported this position. Since August 1940, they had been listening to CBS newsman Edward R. Murrow's nightly radio broadcasts from London. Air-raid sirens wailing and bombs bursting throughout Murrow's live reports brought the Battle of Britain into their homes.

▼ The country's gross national product (GNP)—a measure of economic output—dropped by almost half between 1930 and the Depression's worst year, 1933. Not until 1939 was the GNP securely at the 1930 level again. Soon after, the wartime boom took hold, and the GNP more than doubled.

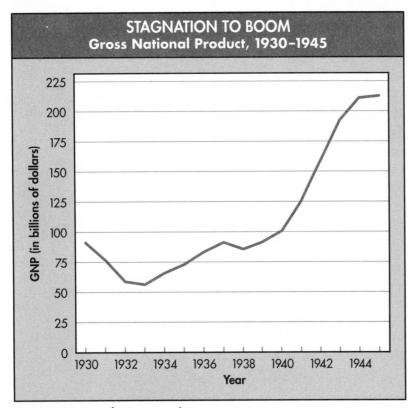

STAGNATION TO BOOM
Gross National Product, 1930–1945

GNP (in billions of dollars) / Year

Source: U.S. Bureau of Economic Analysis.

Meanwhile, in the Pacific, Japan was flexing its military muscle. It invaded Manchuria, a province of China, in 1931 and took Shanghai in 1937. The latter move prompted Roosevelt to ask for, and receive, congressional trade restrictions against Japan. Next, Japan signed military agreements with Germany and Italy in 1940 and took over oil-rich Indochina in 1941.

Fearing for the safety of the Philippines and other U.S. interests in Asia, Roosevelt seized all Japanese financial interests in the United States. He appealed directly to Emperor Hirohito to halt Japan's aggression in Asia. The United States was too distracted by Hitler's march through Europe, however, to pay close attention to Japan's ultimate goal—to remove non-Asian influence from Asia and the Pacific. It was not a new idea. For almost a decade, Japanese naval instructors had been asking their students how they would carry out a surprise attack on Pearl Harbor, in Hawaii. On the morning of December 7, 1941, they demonstrated their answer.

UNCLE SAM GOES TO WAR

Japan's surprise attack on Pearl Harbor on December 7, 1941, ended America's neutrality. Immediately, President Roosevelt asked Congress to declare war on Japan, which it did within one day. In his speech, the president called December 7, 1941, "a date which will live in infamy." Three days later Germany and Italy, honoring their agreement with Japan, declared war on the United States. America was now an active participant in two arenas of a great world war. (See The World for full coverage of World War II.)

Japan's bombing raid at Pearl Harbor united the country as never before. Prior to the attack, Americans had been divided over U.S. involvement in the war in Europe. While people were willing to send arms and supplies to the embattled British, few were willing to risk American lives for what was seen as a European fight. The direct attack on an American base changed attitudes. The shock Americans felt on December 7, 1941, quickly turned to anger and then to firm determination. Secretary of State Cordell Hull spoke for all Americans when he told a foreign dignitary, "We're going to lick the Hell out of them." Words turned into actions. Long lines of young men formed outside military recruiting offices as Americans mobilized to win the war.

The country's mood was nevertheless solemn. People understood that death and heartache were to follow. New Year's Day of 1942 was a day not of celebration but of reflection; it was declared a National Day of Prayer.

Roosevelt as Commander in Chief

Even before Pearl Harbor, the president had prepared for the likelihood of war. In August 1941 he had participated in a secret three-day meeting aboard a ship off the coast of Newfoundland, Canada.

A. PHILIP RANDOLPH, CIVIL RIGHTS LEADER

When the U.S. defense program began in the fall of 1940, 90 percent of the industries that held government contracts either did not employ black workers or restricted blacks to unskilled jobs. Many black leaders complained to President Roosevelt, but he paid little attention.

The situation changed when A. Philip Randolph, the founding president of a railway union of mostly black workers, threatened to stage a march on Washington. On June 25, 1941, one week before the march was to take place, Roosevelt signed Executive Order 8802. This order forced defense contractors to sign nondiscrimination clauses. It also established the Fair Employment Practices Committee (FEPC) as a way of making sure that government employers did not discriminate against blacks.

Here he met face-to-face with Britain's prime minister, Winston Churchill, for the first time. The two leaders' talks produced the Atlantic Charter, a joint statement of peacetime aims for the future. They forged a warm friendship and reinforced a strong bond between their countries. However, Roosevelt stopped short of committing the United States to the war, much to Churchill's disappointment.

December 7, 1941: "A Date Which Will Live in Infamy"

Before dawn on December 7, 1941, the signal "Climb Mt. Niitaka" was issued. This coded message (meaning "Begin the war") sent 353 Japanese war planes streaking across the brightening sky from their carriers in the North Pacific toward the naval base at Pearl Harbor, Hawaii. At 7:53 A.M. (Hawaiian time) the Japanese attack commander signaled "Tora, tora, tora!" (literally, "Tiger, tiger, tiger," meaning "Surprise attack achieved"). His targets were 96 U.S. vessels nestled in the harbor and all the Army planes at Hickam, Bellows, and Wheeler fields lined up in rows like sitting ducks.

Suddenly, at 7:55 A.M. bombs exploded along "Battleship Row" in the harbor, shattering the Sunday morning silence. Ear-splitting explosions mingled with the scream of air-raid sirens. Huge columns of water from torpedo hits shot into the air. The harbor became an inferno of thick smoke, twisted metal, and burning oil. The boilers and forward magazines of the battleship *Arizona* blew up, sinking the ship and killing 1,000 men aboard. Many men were stunned and did not know what to do. A commander on the U.S.S. *Ramapo* hopelessly shot at the planes with a pistol. During the 110-minute attack, 8 battleships and 3 light cruisers were sunk or damaged and 188

▼ ▼ ▼

"We ... looked all over the harbor and you've never seen anything like it. Just ships on fire everywhere you looked."

—Captain Charles Merdinger, U.S.N.

planes were destroyed and over 150 others damaged. Almost 2,400 Americans were killed. The Japanese attack left the U.S. Pacific Fleet paralyzed.

When news of the attack on Pearl Harbor was released nationwide, Americans were shocked and numb with disbelief. People would remember, always, where they were and what they were doing at that moment. Brigadier General Dwight Eisenhower was awakened by a phone call and rushed to headquarters at Fort Sam Houston to meet his destiny. Young Ensign John F. Kennedy heard the news on a car radio.

Since the war, some historians have argued that Roosevelt knew that an attack would come but let it happen in order to convince the U.S. public to enter the war. A 1962 book by historian Roberta Wohlstetter found evidence that the United States had adequate warning that Pearl Harbor would be bombed but that officials did not properly understand the intelligence data. John Toland's 1982 study backs this finding. Toland also adds the statement of an anonymous seaman who claimed that the Navy knew of the attack in advance.

No firm proof has ever been found that Roosevelt knew of the planned strike or that he was consciously trying to manipulate the country into war. But there is no question that the effect of the attack was to unify public opinion.

Once the country was in the war, however, Roosevelt moved swiftly to arm America and forge stronger ties to the **Allies**. As commander in chief of the armed forces he had powers that went far beyond those of normal presidential authority. His one aim was to bring a speedy end to the war. Toward that goal he enlisted the help of all Americans.

The Home Front

Throughout the war, the United States retained an exceptional ability to finance the war effort, to produce arms, and to move these arms overseas. At a meeting of Allied leaders in 1943, Soviet premier Joseph Stalin acknowledged that without American production the Allies would lose the war. By 1944 the country was manufacturing 40 percent of all the world's arms—as well as providing consumer goods in greater amounts. There was full employment, business prospered, and more people were better off than ever before.

Men, women, and children all across the nation went on a giant scavenger hunt, collecting scrap metal, rubber, and paper to add to the raw materials for defense production. Empty toothpaste tubes, car tires, padlocks, and even women's stockings went into the manufacture of war materiel. Victory gardens sprang up everywhere as families grew their own vegetables so farmers could supply the troops.

To help finance the war, the government sold War Bonds. Patriotic citizens bought bonds to the tune of $135 billion. Congress also took a radical new step with

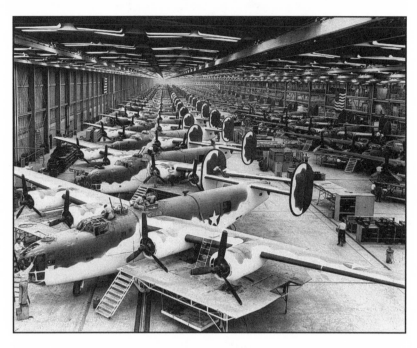

income taxes. Taxes began to be withheld from workers' paychecks. Fear of another attack, this time on the mainland, led to the formation of the Office of Civil Defense. By 1943, 9 million civilian volunteers were serving as spotters scanning the skies for enemy aircraft, and as air-raid wardens checking to see that all houses were blacked out when air-raid sirens sounded. Coastal cities were dark at night. Fear of attack by submarines or planes led city leaders to order building lights turned off.

Americans also had to make some sacrifices. As early as January 1942 the government began **rationing** gas and certain foods, such as meat, sugar, coffee, and butter. Clothing, especially footwear, was often in short supply. With auto manufacturers building trucks and tanks, drivers had to make do with their old cars. Unlike the case in World War I, this rationing was compulsory, or required.

▲ Workers—many of them women—put finishing touches on B-24s, some of which are painted with camouflage. Arms production shot up dramatically, fulfilling FDR's promise to make the country the "arsenal of democracy."

Women During the War

Women were vital to America's wartime success. When men headed off to fight, women took over many factory jobs as welders, riveters, and assemblers. Their enthusiastic support made them symbols for achievement on the home front. About 3.5 million women were working in American industry by 1944, helping to increase production to an all-time high.

Women also served in the armed services. In 1942, the secretary of war authorized a Women's Army Corps (the WACs). The Navy and other branches of the military soon had their own women's corps. The press and men in uniform often poked fun at "soldiers in skirts," yet the women effectively replaced men who were needed on the battlefields. Over 300,000 women worked in the military as clerks, typists, and truck drivers. And it was women auxiliary pilots who flew most of the planes across the Atlantic from U.S. arms factories to Allied bomber and fighter squadrons in Britain.

Black Americans Advance

Black Americans had increasingly moved to the South during the jobless Depression. With the war, however, more moved to the North and West. They could not escape injustice and prejudice, however. Race riots broke out in several cities from Detroit to Los Angeles in the early 1940s.

In early 1941, blacks pressured Roosevelt to ensure equal opportunity in defense industry hiring and to desegregate the armed forces. They threatened a march on Washington to make their point. In response, FDR issued an executive order creating the Fair Employment Practices Commission, which was supposed to investigate any discrimination in hiring. The measure was a major turnaround. It opened factory doors to black workers for the first time. Blacks fought with distinction during the war. About 8,000 black servicemen achieved officer's rank, and the all-black Ninety-ninth Fighter Squadron earned distinguished combat honors.

Blacks joined the National Association for the Advancement of Colored People (NAACP) in record numbers during the war years. In 1942 an interracial group founded the Congress of Racial Equality (CORE), which promoted nonviolent action to achieve equality. In this period CORE staged the first sit-ins against discrimination. CORE would become a national force for the civil rights movement of the 1960s.

America's Shame

After the bombing of Pearl Harbor, Japanese-Americans suffered terribly. Americans ridiculed Japanese people in propaganda. Soon, this widespread racism was directed toward Americans of Japanese descent.

There were only about 127,000 Japanese-Americans in 1941, most of them living in California. Anti-Asian groups spread rumors that Japanese-Americans might bomb oil refineries or spy for their "homeland." The public outcry grew so great that on February 19, 1942, President Roosevelt signed an order that allowed the army to "in-

BIRTHS . . .

Neil Armstrong, astronaut, 1930

Sandra Day O'Connor, Supreme Court justice, 1930

Edward Kennedy, politician, 1932

Gloria Steinem, feminist, 1934

Jesse Jackson, politician, 1941

. . . AND DEATHS

William Howard Taft, president, 1930

Thomas Alva Edison, inventor, 1931

Calvin Coolidge, president, 1933

Jane Addams, social worker, 1935

George Washington Carver, scientist, 1943

tern" all Japanese-Americans living near "military areas" of the West Coast. Over 110,000 ethnic Japanese—70,000 of them American citizens—were moved to ten specially built "relocation centers" in western deserts. They lived in tar-paper shacks surrounded by barbed wire and watchtowers. Many people were held for more than two years. It was a sorry chapter in American history.

The Election of 1944

Roosevelt chose to run for yet another term as president, using the slogan "Don't change horses in midstream." The economy was running smoothly, and the war had definitely turned in favor of the Allies by then. Roosevelt's opponent, Thomas E. Dewey, was a respected businessman and champion of law and order, but he could not shake people's faith in Roosevelt's leadership. FDR was victorious for the fourth time.

The End of an Era

Roosevelt was looking beyond the end of the war when he began shaping his policies early in 1945. He planned to focus again on education, health, and other social issues. But before he could initiate any such programs, he died of a stroke on April 12, 1945. Vice President Harry S. Truman was suddenly thrust into the presidency. It was he who would handle the end of the war and postwar planning.

Americans mourned the death of their longtime leader. For many Americans, he was the only president they had known. Roosevelt had brought the nation through two crises—the Great Depression

and World War II—with strength, courage, and confidence. His New Deal programs introduced the greatest economic and social changes the country had yet experienced. He had extended the power of the presidency and changed the way people looked at the federal government. His humanity and cooperative spirit came to symbolize the values of the American people. Even in the 1980s, more than half the American people rated Roosevelt as one of the three greatest presidents in history (along with Washington and Lincoln).

At his death Roosevelt was working on a speech. One of its lines reveals the man and the leader: "We have learned in the agony of war that great power involves great responsibility. . . . The only limit to our realization of tomorrow will be our doubts of today. Let us move forward with strong and active faith."

▲ Shown here at the Yalta meeting late in World War II are the three main leaders of the Allies (from left): Britain's Winston Churchill, FDR, and the Soviet Union's Joseph Stalin. Churchill and FDR were friendly and cooperative with each other. Relations with Stalin were generally tense.

THE WORLD

The Depression struck throughout the world. Unemployment plagued the nations of Western Europe. Germans also suffered from the sting of their defeat in World War I and the harsh terms of the peace that followed. Into this turmoil came Adolf Hitler, shown above at one of his mass rallies. A ruthless dictator and vicious persecutor of those he called his enemies, Hitler achieved power in Germany by appealing to the national pride and frustration of the German people.

By rebuilding his country's army, navy, and air force, Hitler improved Germany's economy. More important, he forged a mighty weapon poised to achieve his plan of conquering Europe. Joined to Hitler were the fascist government of Italy and the military-controlled govern-

AT A GLANCE

▶ Nationalism on the Rise

▶ The Gathering Storm

▶ Blitzkrieg

▶ Operation Barbarossa

▶ The Allies Strike Back

▶ The Last Days of Hitler

▶ The War in the Pacific

ment of Japan. These three powers invaded neighboring lands and plunged the world into a war more terrible than the Great War earlier in the century. Truly a global conflict, World War II brought fighting to Europe, Africa, Asia, and the Pacific. The war was devastating to soldiers and civilians alike. Indeed, more civilians than soldiers were killed. Many of those civilians were the victims of unspeakable policies of mass execution.

Allied against these powers were a collection of nations led by Great Britain, the Soviet Union, and the United States. Emerging victorious from this effort, the Soviet Union and the United States rose as the world's two superpowers. But their wartime cooperation would not last during peacetime.

DATAFILE

World Population	1930	1940
Total	2.1 bil.	2.3 bil.
Africa	164 mil.	191 mil.
Asia	1.1 bil.	1.2 bil.
Australia and Oceania	10 mil.	11.1 mil.
Central and South America	108 mil.	130 mil.
Europe	355 mil.	380 mil.
North America	134 mil.	144 mil.
USSR	179 mil.	195 mil.

WORLD WAR II CASUALTIES
Military and Civilian Deaths for Selected Countries

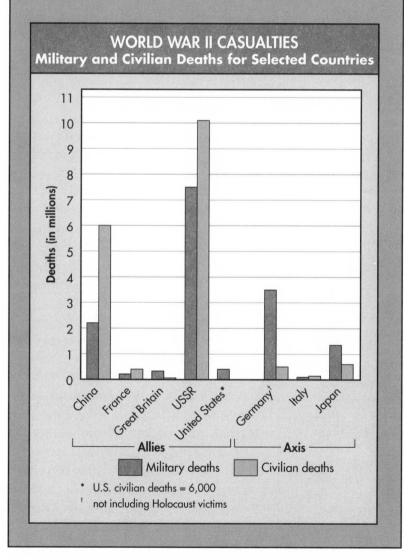

Deaths (in millions)

Allies: China, France, Great Britain, USSR, United States*
Axis: Germany†, Italy, Japan

■ Military deaths   ■ Civilian deaths

* U.S. civilian deaths = 6,000
† not including Holocaust victims

NATIONALISM ON THE RISE

The Depression of the 1930s hit not just the United States but also the entire world. Like the United States, the powerful European democracies followed a policy of **isolationism** as they tried to cope. In Europe's African, Asian, and Middle Eastern colonies, the economic and political pressures of the time stirred waves of **nationalism.** Colonial peoples tried several different methods in their drives for independence. The end of colonialism was near. Independence movements were delayed by the war but then—in that war's aftermath—accelerated.

India and Southeast Asia

Indian nationalist Mohandas (Mahatma) Gandhi was the most important leader of India's independence movement. In 1930 Gandhi and 78 followers violated Britain's salt-tax law when they marched 241 miles to the Arabian Sea and took tax-free salt from its waters. This "Salt March" began a widespread boycott of British goods and mass civil disobedience. People all over India simply stopped buying British products and obeying British laws. By 1935 Britain agreed to the Government of India Act, which gave almost complete self-government to the Indian provinces. Indians, however, continued to press for independence.

Groups in each of the countries of Southeast Asia demanded independence from their colonial rulers

Mohandas K. Gandhi, India's political, social, and spiritual leader for two decades, began a campaign to help the untouchables of his land. These members of India's lowest caste, a legalized social division, had for years been denied the same rights as other citizens.

During 1932 and 1933, Gandhi undertook four fasts to draw attention to the untouchables' plight. Gandhi called the untouchables *harijan*, or "children of God." His fasting helped to secure them voting rights and employment. Gandhi also established a newspaper called *Harijan* that gave untouchables a public voice.

during the 1930s. The Philippines came closest to success. In 1934 the U.S. Congress passed a law promising the Philippines self-government on July 4, 1936, and total independence in 1946. The United States would control defense and foreign affairs and maintain military forces on the island between those years.

Independence movements were also active in Malaya, Burma, and the Netherlands East Indies (Indonesia). They had some limited success until Japan's occupation of these countries in 1942 halted all progress. In French Indochina, Ho Chi Minh founded the Indochinese Communist party in 1930 to fight French rule. By 1941 Ho had combined the Nationalist party

and the Communist party into the Viet Minh, which continued the fight. (The United States would confront these Viet Minh forces several decades later.)

Africa and the Middle East

Revolts against French rule in the North African colonies of French Morocco, Tunisia, and Algeria after World War I did not bring these colonies freedom. But strong nationalist groups were formed, and they continued to press for independence. In the British colony of Kenya, a peaceful freedom movement began in the 1930s. As a whole, however, the European countries kept control of Africa. The African colonies did not achieve independence until the 1950s and 1960s.

In the Middle East many countries did become independent during the 1930s. Iraq gained independence from Britain in 1930, as Yemen did in 1934. The Kingdom of Saudi Arabia was established in 1932. Britain gave Egypt independence in 1936 but retained the right to keep forces near the Suez Canal for defense. During the war, Egypt became the main Allied base in the region.

The territories of Transjordan and Palestine, originally part of the Ottoman Empire, had been created and put under British control after World War I. Transjordan was granted partial self-government in 1921 and gained full independence as the country of Jordan in 1946. The British had trouble in Palestine, though. The region's Arab population fought Britain's policy of allowing Jews to immigrate to Palestine. The Jewish population

Edward VIII Gives Up Throne for Woman He Loves

Edward David Windsor literally gave away his kingdom for love. To the horror of the British aristocracy and the delight of those who had followed the king's storybook romance, he publicly renounced his throne on December 11, 1936. Millions listened to Edward's brief and moving radio speech as he declared that he could not remain king "without the help and support of the woman I love." That woman was Wallis Simpson, an American who had been divorced. In this age, those traits were considered objectionable—at least for a queen.

Edward and Wallis, who was recently divorced for a second time, moved to France, where they soon married. Despite their attempts to avoid the spotlight, the duke and duchess of Windsor were to remain in the public eye until their deaths.

thought the British favored the Arabs. In 1939 Britain agreed to end Jewish immigration by 1944 and to grant independence to Palestine by 1954. However, the situation changed. Hostilities increased between Palestinian Arabs and Jews from 1943 onward. Then came the news of the suffering of Jews in Germany's death camps. In 1947 Palestine was divided into Arab and Jewish zones.

Lebanon achieved independence from France in 1944. Syria did so in 1946, after years of riots and strikes by Syrian nationalists. Turkey became an independent republic as early as 1924. During the 1930s, the Turks followed a policy of modernization and westernization under the leadership of Kemal Atatürk ("father of the Turks"). By expanding education and industry and giving women the right to vote, Atatürk brought Turkey into the modern world.

Latin America

On the heels of prosperity from the 1920s, Latin America suffered economic crisis and increasing social problems during the 1930s. Many democratic governments fell to dictatorships, such as those of Trujillo in the Dominican Republic and Somoza in Nicaragua. However, new agreements and cultural exchanges improved relations between the United States and Latin American countries.

The cornerstone of U.S. policy toward Latin America was the Good Neighbor policy proposed by President Franklin D. Roosevelt in his first inaugural address. He described a good neighbor as one who "respects himself and, because he does so, respects the rights of others." As part of this policy, the United States joined the other nations of America in pledging never to interfere in the affairs of another country. As a result, the United States ended its military occupations of Nicaragua in 1933 and Haiti in 1934. At an inter-American conference in 1936, the countries pledged to consult each other whenever war threatened. The Declaration of Lima (1938) called for American nations to work together in an overall security system. This step gave added strength to hemispheric unity.

U.S.-CUBAN RELATIONS IMPROVE

As part of its Good Neighbor policy, the United States began smoothing relations with Cuba. In May 1934, the two nations signed a treaty revoking the Platt Amendment, which had been part of Cuba's constitution since 1901.

This amendment had given the United States the right to intervene in Cuba's domestic and foreign affairs. Cubans had resented it since its adoption. Once the Platt Amendment was rescinded, the United States could no longer restrict Cuba's right to make treaties or assume debts.

Nobel Peace Prize Winners, 1930-1945

1930	Nathan Söderblom	Swedish archbishop
1931	Jane Addams	American social reformer, peace activist, and founder of Hull House
	Nicholas Murray Butler	American educator
1932	Not awarded	——
1933	Norman Angell	English author and peace activist
1934	Arthur Henderson	English labor leader and statesman
1935	Carl von Ossietzky	German author and pacifist
1936	Carlos Saavedra Lamas	Argentine statesman
1937	Robert Cecil	English statesman
1938	Nansen International Office for Refugees	——
1939	Not awarded	——
1940	Not awarded	——
1941	Not awarded	——
1942	Not awarded	——
1943	Not awarded	——
1944	International Committee of the Red Cross	——
1945	Cordell Hull	American statesman

The Good Neighbor policy worked well. It helped pave the way for good relations in the Western Hemisphere during the war. By renouncing interference, the United States promoted cooperation.

Eastern Europe

War debts and unstable currencies in the Eastern European countries caused economic hardship right after World War I. Conditions only worsened when the global depression of the 1930s hit. In addition, many Jews and other ethnic groups suffered as minorities within the new nations established after the war. Persecution of racial, ethnic, and religious minorities increased throughout Eastern Europe. The problems reached crisis stages in Czechoslovakia, Yugoslavia, and Romania. In Romania an **anti-Semitic** group called the "Iron Guard" gained great power.

Hungary and Bulgaria wanted to recover territory they had lost after World War I. Romania, Yugoslavia, Greece, and Turkey hoped to ward off foreign aggression by forming a loose alliance called the "Balkan Entente." A series of treaties between Czechoslovakia, Romania, and Yugoslavia attempted to form a regional bloc, called the "Little Entente." Its purpose was to keep out German **fascism** and Russian communism and to maintain regional stability.

Eastern Europe, however, was anything but stable. Its alliances were weak. Some countries suffered the rise of dictators, adding to economic and social woes. Overall, the region was ripe for Hitler's plans for conquest and claims of racial supremacy.

THE GATHERING STORM

The 1930s were a turbulent and ominous time. Ruthless dictators—Hitler, Mussolini, and Franco—seized power, each taking steps that helped push the world toward war. They were able to rise at home by appealing to their peoples' strong feelings of nationalism and frustration over the Depression. They used **propaganda** to feed on people's fears and dreams. When that did not work, they resorted to force and terror. Not content with ruling their own nations, they began to search for yet more land. But the Western democracies did not challenge them for many years.

Meanwhile, Japan was building up its military might. Its leaders were planning to conquer neighboring lands to get natural resources needed to improve Japan's poor economy. Around the world, tension was building.

The Spanish Civil War

The tension erupted first in Spain. The Spanish had formed a republican government in 1931. Leaders of the new government started a series of democratic reforms, but the changes drew many opponents. In 1936, Spanish voters reelected the Popular Front, the Republican party leaders of the government. Spanish fascists, the Front's strongest opponents, reacted with more frequent and more violent protests. Several assassinations of army officers followed, as well as a revolt.

Soon Spain was plunged into a bitter civil war. On one side were the Republicans; on the opposing side were the so-called Nationalists, led by General Francisco Franco. The conflict was bloody, lasting three painful years until 1939. The Republicans lost; Franco became dictator.

Spain's civil war had turned international when several foreign countries took sides to further their own interests. Italy and Germany supported Franco's Nationalists; the Soviet Union sent troops to aid the Republicans. But the United States remained neutral, and Britain and France refused to answer the Republicans' plea for aid. Volunteers from these and other countries formed an International Brigade and went to Spain to fight for the Republicans. But the organized support of the fascist dictators proved stronger.

The Spanish Civil War strengthened ties between Italy and Germany. It also provided the growing German war machine with a chance to test its weapons and tactics. Neutrality made France and Britain appear unwilling to act in support of their beliefs and interests. The war was an omen of what was to come on a global scale.

Italy Under Mussolini

"Blood," Benito Mussolini said, "moves the wheel of history." He made sure there was enough blood spilled to keep the wheel turning. Mussolini rose to power in Italy not through elections but by beatings, terror, and murder. He led Europe's first fascist government. In fact, Mussolini coined the word *fascist,* which came from the word for an ancient Roman symbol of power. By 1930 Mussolini had

been in power for eight years. He had restored Italy's self-confidence and established the "corporate state," which meant he controlled both the government and the economy. Appealing to people's fears and prejudices, he promised to protect Italy from communism and to revive the glories of ancient Rome. Although he had modernized the railroad system and given workers some help, Mussolini made few domestic reforms. Instead, he created the appearance of progress by using a tool more subtle than terror—propaganda.

In the thirties Mussolini began an aggressive foreign policy aimed at creating a new Roman Empire. To that end he invaded Ethiopia in 1935. The world powers did nothing. The League of Nations merely called on nations to cut off trade with Italy. Without help, Ethiopia quickly fell to Mussolini and became known as Italian East Africa.

In 1937 Mussolini signed the Anti-Comintern Pact with Germany

▼ Mussolini used propaganda to generate support in mass rallies like this one. When the Allies invaded Italy, the propaganda failed and he tried to flee the country. Italians showed their anger at the suffering his war had brought them by capturing and killing him.

VOLKSWAGEN BEETLE DEBUTS IN GERMANY

On February 6, 1936, the Volkswagen ("people's car") was born. This German car was designed by Ferdinand Porsche to be inexpensive enough for the average family to own.

The car—called the "Beetle"—was not put into large-scale production until after World War II. To keep manufacturing costs low, the company decided to produce this one model without yearly changes. Its design, like Henry Ford's Model T, was simple, and the car cost little to operate and maintain. Although many people ridiculed the Beetle as ugly and slow, the car was very popular all over the world.

More than 19 million Beetles were produced until the car was discontinued in 1978, making it the best-selling model in history.

▶ Stalin shifted alliances during the period, signing an agreement with Hitler in 1939 and then joining the Allies when Germany invaded his country. Britain's Winston Churchill summed up his mistrust of Stalin by calling Russia—and thus Stalin—"a riddle wrapped in a mystery inside an enigma."

and Japan, which declared communism to be the three nations' mutual enemy. During the Spanish Civil War, Mussolini sent almost 75,000 troops to aid Franco's fascist Nationalists. This move linked him more closely to Nazi Germany, even though he opposed Hitler's anti-Semitic racial theories. But the link to Germany had benefits, it seemed. When Germany invaded Czechoslovakia in 1939, Mussolini moved to **annex** Albania.

The "Stalin Revolution"

As dictator of the Soviet Union from 1929 to 1953, Joseph Stalin created the ultimate **totalitarian** state. Ruthless and suspicious, he would not tolerate any disagreement or criticism of his views or

policies. During his reign, millions of Soviet citizens were killed or sent to labor camps in the barren wastelands of Siberia. Stalin made terror a state institution. He created a concentration camp system that rivaled Hitler's in Germany. Where Hitler ordered the deaths of millions out of ethnic hatred, Stalin's purpose was simply to maintain his power.

Stalin consolidated his power and put his domestic and foreign plans into action between 1929 and 1939, a decade referred to as the "Stalin Revolution." By the end of it, he had **nationalized** all industry, introduced rapid industrial growth, and put all business and banking under state control. Indeed, he had taken control of Soviet society in general. He also forced peasants off their small farm plots and onto large state-owned **collective farms**. There they produced crops and livestock according to government planning. The state's plans failed, however. Agricultural production dropped and famine struck in 1932 and 1933.

Some opponents of Stalin within the Communist party started a secret movement to remove him from power. But their plot became known after the murder of a party official in 1934. Stalin responded with a five-year-long **purge**. High-ranking political and military officers were executed, and about 10 million Soviet citizens were sent to labor camps.

In foreign affairs, Stalin tried to protect his country from the worrisome aims of Germany and Japan. In 1939, he shocked many throughout the world by signing a pact with Hitler in which both leaders agreed not to attack each other. The pact also stated that Germany and the USSR would divide Eastern Europe between them. Thus, when Germany attacked Poland that same year, the Soviet Union invaded Finland. In 1940, Stalin went on to annex the Baltic states of Latvia, Estonia, and Lithuania.

Stalin took the same approach with his eastern neighbors. Fights with the Japanese broke out along the Manchurian border in 1938. But in 1941 Stalin and Japan's leaders agreed not to attack each other or take part in each other's foreign conflicts. Stalin had signed treaties with two of his country's most bitter enemies. The USSR now seemed safe.

The Third Reich

The bloodiest and most terrible fascist of them all arose in the ashes of defeated Germany. By 1930 Germany was in an economic crisis beyond the control of its democratic government. Nor could the government cope with the violence of such groups as the Brownshirts, street bullies who used force to further the cause of the newly formed Nazi party—the party of Adolf Hitler.

The Nazi, or National Socialist, party was one of many extremist movements formed in the turbulent 1920s in Germany. It first reached national attention by attempting to seize the government of a German province. The attempt failed, and Hitler was sent to prison. Once released, Hitler got the party moving again. His speeches began to have growing appeal among the many jobless.

He also got support from the military and German nationalists, bitter over the harsh conditions of the Treaty of Versailles.

When the Nazis were voted a parliamentary majority in 1933, Hitler was named chancellor, or prime minister. He moved swiftly to remove opposition by banning all political parties except his own. He declared himself *Führer*, or leader, and proclaimed that Germany was now the Third Reich ("empire"). He promised the Germans a national rebirth, in which the world would follow the lead of the Germans, whom he considered part of a superior Aryan race.

Hitler used propaganda to inflame Germans against their "enemies"—the communists, the socialists, homosexuals, and Gypsies. Most of all, he attacked the Jews. He formed the Gestapo ("secret police") to squelch protest and help persecute the Jews. Hitler made his first move against the Jews in 1935 with the passage of the Nuremberg Laws, which forbade non-Jews from marrying or conducting business with Jews. Violence against Jews increased and culminated in *Kristallnacht* ("night of broken glass") in November 1938, a nationwide attack on Jewish property.

Hitler had other plans to pursue as well. To revive Germany's economy, Hitler rebuilt the nation's army, navy, and air force. This step violated the Treaty of Versailles, but Hitler did not care. Other nations protested; Hitler ignored them. The economy rebounded—by 1937 unemployment was low, and the German war machine was ready to roll.

KRISTALLNACHT— A NIGHT OF TERROR

On the night of November 9, 1938, Nazis unleashed their first major action against European Jews. The night is now known as *Kristallnacht,* which is German for "crystal night," or "night of broken glass." The name refers to the shattered windows of shops and homes that the Nazis left behind.

Kristallnacht was ordered by Adolf Hitler on the excuse that a German diplomat had recently been shot by a Polish-Jewish student in Paris. In a single night, 91 Jews were killed, hundreds more were seriously injured, and countless thousands were terrorized. The Nazis also burned about 177 synagogues and destroyed 7,500 Jewish-owned businesses. During the violence, police were not allowed to interfere with the Nazis or aid the Jews in any way.

Kristallnacht was followed by the arrest of 30,000 Jewish men, who were later sent to Nazi concentration camps. Today, people across the world remember *Kristallnacht* by holding candlelight vigils, religious services, and discussions of that night and its consequences.

With Germany stronger, Hitler moved to achieve the goal he had stated in his book *Mein Kampf* ("my struggle"). That goal was to make Germany a world power by getting *Lebensraum* ("living space") in Eastern Europe. First Hitler withdrew Germany from the League of Nations. Then, to disguise his real intentions, he signed a nonaggression pact with Poland and a naval pact with Britain, which limited the size of the German navy. By 1936 he had signed a friendship agreement with Mussolini, forming the Berlin-Rome Axis. In 1938 he annexed Austria, thus achieving his goal of bringing the ethnic Germans of Austria into the Reich. His next steps would bring Europe closer to war.

Land of the Rising Sun

Yet one more aggressive power was rising on the scene, and that was in the East. Japan, which depended on foreign trade, was hit especially hard by the worldwide

Adolf Hitler: A "Monster of Wickedness"

How could such an undistinguished man as Adolf Hitler—with his enormous ego, slight intellectual ability, and complete lack of morality and humanity—gain total control over Germany, conquer most of Europe, and bring the world to the edge of chaos? In 1941 British prime minister Churchill described him as a "monster of wickedness" whose "Nazi gangsters" rolled their "military machine" onward, "grinding up human lives."

Adolf Hitler (1889–1945) possessed an evil political genius along with a conviction that he was to play a historic role as Germany's savior. He understood the weaknesses of his opponents, was willing to take risks, and could bend others to his will.

During his calculated rise to power, Hitler gained public support by appealing to people's fears, prejudices, and desire to dominate. His greatest talent was as a speaker; he roused his audiences' emotions, often driving them into a frenzy. His speaking style consisted of repeating key points in the simplest language possible and making emotionally charged attacks against his enemies. Hitler made the army swear a personal loyalty oath to him. He demanded complete and unquestioning obedience.

▼▼▼

"The great masses of the people will more easily fall victims to a big lie than to a small one."

—Adolf Hitler

Hitler expressed his political and social ideas in his book *Mein Kampf,* written while he was in prison. He wrote of the destiny of the German people. He claimed that Germans needed a strong leader to return them to supremacy in Europe and to help them gain "living space" by acquiring needed territory in the east. The book was full of anti-Semitism. Hitler blamed Jewish people for Germany's defeat in World War I and pledged to purify the German race by getting rid of all Jews. He attempted to prove "scientifically" that the Jews were inferior and the source of all corruption.

Hitler's methods for achieving his ends were also revealed throughout the book. "Strength lies not in defense, but in attack," he wrote, and "the one means that wins the easiest victory over reason: terror and force." He fulfilled these menacing promises.

depression. Many other countries placed high tariffs on Japanese goods, which cut into Japan's needed export sales. The poor economy led to social and political unrest.

In the chaos, military leaders gained control of the government. They planned to solve the economic crisis by conquering neighboring countries in Asia and seizing their resources. In 1931 the Japanese invaded the Chinese province of Manchuria. President Roosevelt protested and the League of Nations condemned the act, but no one tried to stop it. In 1932, Japan annexed Manchuria and built iron and steel mills and a military base there. A year later, Japan withdrew from the League.

In 1937 Japanese soldiers clashed with Chinese soldiers near Beijing (Peking). Japan then went on to invade China. The following year Japan announced that it would expel all non-Asian interests, including those of the United States and Britain, from the Pacific region. In its place would be a new Asian community with Japan at the helm. The world moved yet another step closer to war.

BLITZKRIEG

"England has been offered a choice between war and shame. She has chosen shame—and will get war." Winston Churchill was speaking in Parliament in outrage over his country's failure to stand up to Hitler's latest demands. Once

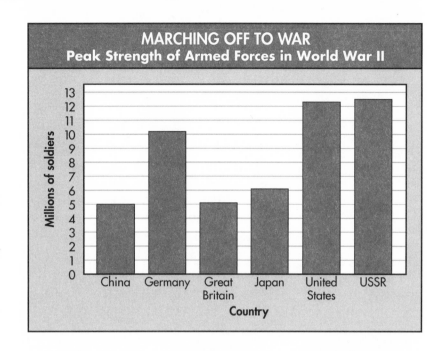

MARCHING OFF TO WAR
Peak Strength of Armed Forces in World War II

Hitler had annexed Austria, he moved to absorb the Sudetenland, a region of western Czechoslovakia that was home to 3 million ethnic Germans. The situation became critical in 1938. To resolve the dispute, the leaders of Britain and France met in Munich with Hitler and Mussolini. There they agreed to give a large part of Czechoslovakia to Hitler along with some areas of Poland and Hungary. Hitler promised to claim no more land. Only a few disorganized provinces remained independent. It was this abandonment of Czechoslovakia that had aroused Churchill's wrath.

By agreeing to Hitler's demands, Britain and France followed a policy of appeasement—giving in to avoid war. It was a policy doomed to failure. Prime Minister Neville Chamberlain told the British people upon his return, "I believe it is peace for our time." But the next year it became clear that Chamberlain was wrong and Churchill was right.

▲ The graph shows the maximum size of each of the major combatants' armies. By the end of the war, Germany was barely able to raise soldiers—who were needed to replace the country's growing losses on two fronts.

The Invasion of Poland

By March 1939 German troops had taken all, not just part, of Czechoslovakia. Britain and France expressed shock, but again they took no action. That same month Hitler demanded that Poland give up the city of Danzig and allow Germany to build road and rail lines across Polish territory. The lines would give Germany direct links with its province of East Prussia, which was separated from the rest of the Reich. Poland refused, with Britain and France promising to support Poland if Germany invaded. European nations now knew that Hitler could not be trusted. He was ready to extend territorial claims beyond his stated goal of uniting areas with German populations.

After Italy annexed Albania, Hitler wanted to cement relations with Italy. In May 1939 he signed the Pact of Steel with Mussolini, promising mutual support in any war. Then he made an ideological turnabout that signaled Poland's end. After years of anticommunist speeches, Hitler signed a pact with Stalin. Germany and the Soviet Union pledged not to fight. Hitler had removed the threat of the only power capable of thwarting his plans for Poland.

On September 1, 1939, the German Luftwaffe, or air force, bombed Poland while German tanks and motorized infantry swept into the country. The blitzkrieg ("lightning war") had begun. The Poles fought valiantly, but Polish men on horseback with lances and swords were no match for German tanks. After eleven days of German bombardment, Warsaw fell. Meanwhile, Russian troops had invaded Poland from the east. Squeezed on both sides, Poland was completely crushed by October 6. Germany and the Soviet Union divided the country according to their deal.

An outraged Britain and France declared war on Germany on September 3, 1939, but no significant fighting took place for several months. In the spring of 1940 Germany captured Norway in a daring naval assault. German armies also occupied Denmark through a land

▼ German soldiers move to occupy yet another Polish city destroyed by air bombardment. German tactics stunned the world. The coordinated use of air power and armored divisions gave the military edge to the attacker, breaking the defensive pattern of World War I.

and sea invasion. These countries were of great strategic importance to the Reich.

The Fall of France

In the spring of 1940 the Germans struck to the west. They smashed through neutral Belgium and the Netherlands, drove British troops from continental Europe, and brought France to its knees. Their war strategy relied on secrecy, speed, surprise, and the power of tanks and planes. The Germans also had daring plans, such as using gliders to land troops on a Belgian fort or disguising Germans as Dutch soldiers to capture a bridge.

Hitler also outwitted British and French forces, who were preparing for battle near the coast, by sending his panzer (tank) divisions through Luxembourg and overrunning France from the north. In so doing, Hitler trapped the British army in France between his advancing forces and the sea. Between May 27 and June 4, about 350,000 men were evacuated in hundreds of little ships from the beaches at Dunkirk to the safety of Britain. Civilians in fishing boats, barges, ferries, and anything that could float braved the constant German artillery fire and air attacks to rescue the troops. The "Miracle of Dunkirk" showed British determination and became a psychological victory for Britain.

But the reality for France was a bitter one. On June 14 the German army marched down Paris's main avenue, the Champs-Élysées, and raised the Nazi flag on the Eiffel Tower. The French stood in stunned silence and wept. The Germans overran most of France and,

after signing an armistice with the French government, set up a puppet government with Vichy as its capital city. Now Britain stood alone to face Hitler's fury.

The Battle of Britain

On June 18, 1940, Prime Minister Churchill told Parliament: "I expect that the Battle of Britain is about to begin. . . . Hitler knows that he will have to break us in this island or lose the war. . . . Let us therefore . . . so bear ourselves that, if the British Empire . . . last[s] for a thousand years, men will still say, 'This was their finest hour.'" Chamberlain had resigned, his appeasement policy putting him in disgrace. In his place the experienced, eloquent, pugnacious Churchill had taken office.

Once again Churchill was right. From July to November 1940, Britain's courage and strength were tested to their limits as Hitler's Luftwaffe rained terror on the country. At first German bombers attacked Britain's harbors and military bases and tried to destroy the Royal Air Force (RAF) and its airstrips. After an RAF bombing raid on Berlin, however, Hitler changed targets. He ordered the Luftwaffe to "raze their cities to the ground." This was a great mistake for Hitler because it gave the RAF time to recover from its losses. Hitler also failed to understand the value of Britain's radar towers because radar was a new technology. By not destroying them, he enabled the British to gather advance warning of German air attacks.

Though good for the RAF, the new German tactic rained fire on the British people. After some fifty

GERMANY'S PANZER DIVISION

One reason for Germany's success in launching the blitzkrieg, or "lightning war," was the panzer division.

Most World War II panzer divisions consisted of two to four battalions of tanks, with smaller backups of motorized infantry and artillery, as well as engineer troops and support services. The tanks' destructive force made it possible for German soldiers to invade in their wake.

FRANCE CONSTRUCTS MAGINOT LINE

The death and destruction of World War I left deep scars on the French countryside and in the hearts of the French people. To protect the country from any future German invasions, the French began in 1930 to build a series of underground forts along the French-German border. These fortifications, stretching for 200 miles, were called the Maginot Line.

The French believed that this defense could never be crossed by invading armies.

The impenetrable Maginot Line had a problem, however—a 50-mile gap in the hills and forests near the French-Belgian border. Once the Germans defeated Belgium, they simply marched into France by going through that gap.

Winston Churchill: Man of the Century

"Winston Churchill was Britain." Thus spoke Dwight Eisenhower in a broadcast at Churchill's funeral in 1965. In 1940, at the age of 65, Churchill became prime minister and led his country through the dark days of the Battle of Britain. He became "the voice that led nations, raised armies, inspired victories, and blew fresh courage into the hearts of men," as another American said at Churchill's death.

The descendant of a British national hero, the first duke of Marlborough, Winston was a self-confident and often rebellious man with an active mind and tremendous courage. By the 1930s he had gained fame as a statesman, writer, speaker, and painter, and as first lord of the admiralty. His insight regarding world events was acute. He warned Britain and the West of "the gathering storm" in Germany while Hitler was rearming and preparing for conquest, but his voice went unheeded.

Churchill became a larger-than-life legend during the war years. He had a genius for leadership that captured the popular imagination, developed loyalty, and inspired devotion. His stooped figure, bulldog face, giant cigar, and two-fingered V-for-victory sign made him instantly recognizable wherever he went. During the London Blitz he walked through the wreckage, urging people on. He never failed to visit the troops to boost their morale.

Churchill was completely involved in strategic planning for Allied invasions and often challenged the military commanders on a proposed course of action. A steady stream of orders flowed from his office, always headed by the command "Action this day." He became close friends with General Eisenhower and President Roosevelt but remained suspicious of Stalin and his postwar objectives.

Probably Churchill's greatest contribution to the war, however, was his ability to inspire. As was said in 1953, when he was awarded the Nobel Prize for literature, he "mobilized" the language. When he became prime minister, Churchill told the nation: "I have nothing to offer but blood, toil, tears, and sweat," but he promised "victory at all costs, victory in spite of all terror, victory however long and hard the road may be; for without victory there is no survival." After the evacuation from Dunkirk, Churchill feared a German invasion of Britain was at hand. He encouraged other worried Britons—and inspired free peoples everywhere in the world—with his eloquent vow: "we shall defend our island, whatever the cost may be, we shall fight on the beaches, we shall fight on the landing grounds, we shall fight in the fields and in the streets, we shall fight in the hills; we shall never surrender."

consecutive nights of targeting London, the Luftwaffe began an intensive bombing campaign, called the "Blitz," on the night of September 7, 1940. A fireman battling smoke and heat early in the onslaught screamed, "The whole bloody world's on fire!" To Londoners the statement must have seemed true. During that night, German bombs destroyed the city's docks and inflicted 3,300 casualties. Hitler hoped that the stepped-up, furious bombing would convince Churchill to sue for peace. The British had held out for nearly two months of raging fires, crumbling buildings, and death in all their cities. But Churchill was not one to give in.

The RAF continued to meet each German assault. As the fall wore on, the outnumbered British pilots inflicted heavy damage on the Germans. The Luftwaffe lost two planes to each one the British lost. Churchill praised the British pilots, saying, "Never in the field of human conflict was so much owed by so many to so few." Although German bombs continued to drop until May 1941, Britain had survived the worst. Hitler abandoned his plans for invading the island and turned eastward instead. It was his next major mistake.

OPERATION BARBAROSSA

Less than two years after agreeing not to fight the Soviet Union, Hitler launched his attack on that na-tion. He had always planned to invade the Soviet Union, wanting the industries and farmlands for Germany's "living space." He also wanted to eliminate a possible rival for power in Europe. His 1939 agreement with Stalin had only been a stalling tactic—and now the time had come. On the night of June 21, 1941, Hitler's Operation Barbarossa, the greatest land war the world has ever known, roared into life. The Germans planned three attack routes: one army group would take the Baltic area, a second would seize the resource-rich lands of the Ukraine and Caucasus, and the third would push toward Moscow.

Hidden in forests and cornfields, more than 3 million men with 600,000 vehicles and 3,350 tanks waited silently along a 1,250-mile frontier from the Baltic to the Black Sea. At 3:15 A.M. they got the signal to move. Thunderous explosions and fireworks shattered the night as thousands of bombs and artillery shots announced the German invasion. The Luftwaffe had already mined the Black and Baltic seas and bombed Soviet airfields. Now they bombed the road ahead of the advancing German army. Soviet defenses were spread too thin and their military was too unprepared to halt the Germans.

Stalin rallied his people by telling them that this was a "national patriotic war." He announced a scorched earth policy, under which the Soviets were to destroy much of their own land, leaving not "a single railway engine, a single wagon, a single pound of grain" for the enemy. The

"*You* ask, what is our policy? I will say: It is to wage war, by sea, land, and air, with all our might and with all the strength that God can give us: to wage war against a monstrous tyranny, never surpassed in the dark, lamentable catalogue of human crime."

—Winston S. Churchill, *Their Finest Hour*

The first meeting between the foes of the Axis powers took place in August 1941, before the United States even entered the war. Roosevelt and Churchill met aboard a ship off Newfoundland and issued the Atlantic Charter, in which they stated their war aims of supporting democracy.

Roosevelt and Churchill next met in Washington in 1942. They decided to concentrate on the fighting in Europe against Hitler.

In January 1943 the two leaders met again in Casablanca as the Allies' North Africa campaign was meeting success. At this meeting, Roosevelt—who favored an early invasion of France—agreed to Churchill's plan to drive the Germans out of Italy first.

In November 1943 the two leaders met with Stalin for the first time. This Teheran meeting resulted in the plans for Britain and the United States to invade France the next year.

The Yalta Conference in February 1945, attended by all three of the leaders, produced plans for the postwar world. The Potsdam Conference later in 1945 confirmed those plans, but Roosevelt had died by then and his place was taken by Harry S. Truman.

people rose to defend "Mother Russia." They followed Stalin's slogan to "stand fast, hold out, and if need be die."

The Fall of Kiev

In the summer of 1941 the Germans captured much of the Ukraine. Their soldiers marched through intense heat, with dust that clogged machinery and made eyes water, and during thunderstorms that turned the roads to mud. When Kiev, the capital of the Ukraine, fell in September, the Germans took the largest number of prisoners in the history of warfare—about 750,000.

During the conquest of the Ukraine, the Nazis committed a horrible act of mass murder. Nazis rounded up some 100,000 Ukrainian Jews, Gypsies, and political prisoners, marched them to the top of the ravine of Babi Yar, and shot them, dumping their bodies into the ravine. In 1943 the Nazis tried to erase evidence of the massacre, but the memory has remained. Babi Yar was a horrifying preview of the mass killings to come.

The Siege of Leningrad

The Germans had planned a quick, surprise attack on Leningrad (renamed Saint Petersburg in 1991), but Hitler decided at the last minute to assault Moscow instead. Thus, on September 15, 1941, the Germans surrounded Leningrad and began a siege. Blocking all entrances to the city, their strategy was to starve the city into surrender during the coming winter.

The suffering was intense, but the people of Leningrad managed to endure. People froze to death because of fuel shortages; they ate rats and other animals for food. The dead lay where they fell, frozen in the snow. When Lake Ladoga froze, however, the besieged citizens were able to drag some supplies across the ice and build a crude road through the forest to meet a railway line. By August 1942 the worst was over—but the siege continued. In the end, the people of Leningrad held out for almost 900 days, until liberated in January 1944.

Moscow: Operation Typhoon

In September 1941 the German army rolled toward Moscow, mowing down all resistance. By October, however, heavy rains slowed movement as wagons and tanks got stuck in knee-deep mud. Then, just 20 miles from the Kremlin, the Soviet capital at Moscow, the Germans were completely halted. Moscow's weapon was no army but rather the fierce Russian winter. Machine guns froze, and more than 14,000 men lost hands, feet, and limbs to frostbite.

Inside the city people had built 60 miles of antitank ditches and 5,000 miles of trenches in preparation for the assault. Stalin, who had remained in the city to boost morale, ordered two Russian counterattacks on the stalled Germans. The Reich forces were pushed back, and Moscow was saved. The Germans still met with some success, however. By July 1942, after an eight-month siege, they captured the Crimean port of Sevastopol, a natural fortress of steep cliffs and the base for the Soviet Black Sea fleet.

The Siege of Stalingrad

His advance checked at Leningrad and Moscow, Hitler began a new offensive. In the summer of 1942 he launched a massive southward push to capture the oil fields of the Caucasus and the industries along the Don River. Victories early in the campaign made Hitler overconfident and prompted him to underestimate the growing strength of the Soviet army. His armies were headed for disaster at the Soviet city of Stalingrad (now Volgograd).

As the German army moved toward the city, Stalin mobilized the people of Stalingrad to build trenches and blockade streets. He ordered the army to hold the city with the words, "Not a step backwards!" The Luftwaffe pounded the city, reducing it to ruins, but the Soviets stayed. When the Germans entered the city, they had to fight for every street, for every ruined building, even for every room, often in hand-to-hand combat. The Soviets perfected techniques for close combat: they wrapped their feet to deaden the sound of footsteps and became expert snipers.

The Germans found the fighting a nightmare, their gains "measured in corpses." On January 31, 1943, after five bloody months of fighting, the German army surrendered. The horror at Stalingrad left 750,000 Russian soldiers and civilians dead. At least 300,000 Germans were killed and another 108,000 taken prisoner. Germany had suffered its first great defeat of World War II. The armies of the Reich were now on the defensive as the Allies struck elsewhere.

THE ALLIES STRIKE BACK

By the end of 1941 both the Soviet Union and the United States had entered the war. It took time, but gradually the **Allies** began inflicting major blows to the Nazi war machine. A challenge for the Allies was to protect the ships carrying war materials from the United States to Europe. Merchant ships crossed the Atlantic Ocean in convoys (large groups), which were guarded by armed escort ships. Even so, from 1940 to early 1942 the German U-boats (submarines) and long-range bombers sank many ships. The tide began to turn, however, when the Allies broke the signal code used by the German U-boat commanders.

Victory at El Alamein

By October 1942 German forces controlled much of the North African coast. Field Marshal Erwin Rommel, called the "Desert Fox,"

▲ Soviet soldiers celebrate the end of the siege of Stalingrad. The Soviet army had counterattacked from two directions, surrounding the Germans in and near the city. Starved and nearly frozen, the Germans finally surrendered at the end of January 1943.

lay in wait for an Allied attack in the desert 60 miles east of Alexandria, Egypt. To stop the Allies, Rommel had prepared the "Devil's Garden," a maze of mines, bombs, barbed wire, and booby traps, outside the village of El Alamein.

Britain's Lieutenant General Bernard Montgomery, "Monty" to his men, had carefully planned the Allied attack. He built a dummy army base in the south to make the Germans think he would attack from there. His real base, however, was in the north. Backed by superior air power and relying on military engineers to sweep the desert for mines and traps, the Allied forces blasted their way through Rommel's complex defenses. Rommel and his famed Afrika Korps retreated, and the Allies recaptured all the territory previously lost, reaching Tripoli in January 1943. The confrontation at El Alamein remains one of history's great turning-point battles.

Warsaw Ghetto Uprising

While the German army suffered defeats in North Africa and at Stalingrad, Hitler pushed ahead with his "Final Solution" to the "Jewish problem." Hundreds of thousands of Jews were taken from the **ghettos** where they lived or the concentration camps where the Germans had placed them. They were sent to death camps, where the Nazis performed mass executions.

Some Jews escaped from the camps and others attempted armed resistance. The Warsaw ghetto uprising in the spring of 1943 became the most celebrated example of Jewish resistance. About 500,000 Jews had been walled off from the rest of the city in 1940, and **deportations** at the rate of 6,000 per day began in July 1942. When the 60,000 Jews left in Warsaw found out that most of

Erwin Rommel: The "Desert Fox"

A daring commander known for his surprise attacks, Germany's field marshal Erwin Rommel (1891–1944) became a national hero in 1942. He had just driven the Allied forces back some 600 miles from Libya to within 60 miles of Alexandria, Egypt. There he captured the Allied stronghold of Tobruk. The German public and press exulted, crowning him "invincible."

As commander of the Afrika Korps of tanks and infantry, Rommel had fought intense heat, blinding sunlight, and swirling sandstorms as well as the Allied forces. Rommel had adapted well to the desert area and quickly found his opponents' weak points. His claim that he could "sniff through the country like a fox" earned him the nickname the "Desert Fox."

Rommel's renowned panzers became a major obstacle to Allied success in North Africa. A frustrated Churchill once angrily said, "Rommel, Rommel, what else matters but beating him." Britain's Lieutenant General Bernard Montgomery, leading the Eighth Army, finally did defeat Rommel in the battle of El Alamein in 1942.

Although Rommel served in other high positions afterward, he never matched his exploits in North Africa. In 1944 he and several other German army officers were discovered plotting to assassinate Hitler. Rommel swallowed poison to avoid execution for treason.

the deported people had been sent to the gas chambers at Treblinka, they decided to fight. The battle lasted 28 days, the Jews using pistols, rifles, and a few grenades against German bombs and machine guns. The Germans reduced the ghetto to rubble, and any Jews left alive were deported. However, 70 of the Jewish fighters escaped through the sewers and joined the Polish resistance.

The Third Reich Stumbles

In November 1942 a massive British-American assault force under the command of General Dwight D. Eisenhower landed on the shores of North Africa. The invasion succeeded, and Eisenhower's troops captured Algeria and Morocco. Next they moved eastward to meet Montgomery and his army in Tunisia. The combined forces squeezed the Axis forces out of North Africa. Although the German-Italian army fought hard, it was forced to surrender. On May 13, 1943, Churchill received the Allied message: "We are the masters of the North African shores."

As the Tunisian campaign got underway in January 1943, Roosevelt and Churchill met in Casablanca, where they decided that the next move would be the invasion of Sicily and Italy. In July 1943, 181,000 men with 14,000 vehicles and 600 tanks under the joint command of Montgomery and U.S. Lieutenant General George S. Patton landed on the southern shores of Sicily. By mid-August they had captured the island and were headed toward mainland Italy. In a key turn of events, Mussolini was ousted from power, and

Italian king Victor Emmanuel sought peace with the Allies. However, the Germans quickly moved troops into Rome and other major areas to continue the fight. The Allies advanced slowly up the

Major Events of the War in Europe

Sept. 1, 1939	Germany invades Poland
May 29–June 4, 1940	British and French troops rescued at Dunkirk
June 14, 1940	German troops occupy Paris
July 1940–May 1941	Battle of Britain
June 22, 1941	Germany invades Soviet Union
Sept. 8, 1941–Jan. 7, 1944	Siege of Leningrad
Nov. 15, 1941	Germany nears Moscow, then stalls; Soviets begin counterattack in December
April 10–Nov. 29, 1941	Battle of Tobruk
Oct. 23–Nov. 4, 1942	Battle of El Alamein
Nov. 8, 1942	Allies land in North Africa
Nov. 19, 1942–Jan. 31, 1943	Battle of Stalingrad
May 1943	Warsaw Ghetto uprising
July 10, 1943	Allies land in Sicily
July 25, 1943	Mussolini resigns
Sept. 3, 1943	Italy surrenders
Sept. 9, 1943	Allies land in mainland Italy
June 4, 1944	Allies take Rome
June 6, 1944	Allies land in Normandy
July 20, 1944	Rebel German generals attempt to assassinate Hitler but fail
Aug. 25, 1944	Allies liberate Paris
Sept. 12, 1944	Allies enter Germany from the west
Oct. 7, 1944	Germany begins V-2 attacks on Britain
Dec. 16, 1944–Jan. 1945	Battle of the Bulge
April 12, 1945	FDR dies; Truman becomes president
April 16–May 2, 1945	Soviet and German troops fight Battle of Berlin
April 25, 1945	U.S. and Soviet troops meet at Torgau, Germany
April 30, 1945	Hitler commits suicide
May 8, 1945	Germany signs surrender at Berlin

The Holocaust: Descent into Hell

Hitler's systematic murder of European Jews was the most barbaric, concentrated attempt at **genocide** in history. From 1933 to 1945 about 6 million Jews died in massacres or from disease, abuse through overwork, or starvation.

The Nazis built concentration camps as early as 1933 to imprison people they considered "enemies of the state," such as religious leaders, political opponents, homosexuals, and Gypsies.

▼ When Allied troops moved into Germany, they found the death camps. Then they learned of the Nazis' barbarity from starving, disease-afflicted survivors like these. Eisenhower summoned congressmen and reporters to hear these stories and get the horrible news to the rest of the world.

Jews were sent to these camps, too. As prisoners arrived, German guards stripped them of all their belongings, tattooed their arms with identifying marks, and shaved their heads. The Germans classified prisoners according to their ethnic background and assigned each group certain colored patches to be worn on striped prison clothing. Jews wore yellow patches.

The Nazis established death camps, the "Final Solution" to the "Jewish problem," by early 1942. Some of these were concentration camps already built; others were new camps. Jews from Germany and the occupied lands were herded like cattle into railroad freight cars and brought to these camps. Prisoners were told they would be taking showers as they were crammed into rooms holding up to 2,000 persons. After locking all doors, camp attendants filled the chamber with a form of cyanide gas or with carbon monoxide. Within 15 minutes all victims inside would be dead. The corpses were then dragged from the gas chambers, searched for gold teeth, and burned in ovens. The Nazis killed as many as 6,000 people a day in these gas chambers. The Nazis also killed Jews through hor-

rible medical "experiments" that were nothing more than torture and murder.

The Nazi regime tried to keep this policy of mass murder secret from the world by locating the death camps in remote areas of Eastern Europe. Not until the Warsaw ghetto uprising in 1943 did the outside world begin to realize what was happening in Germany. In early 1945, Heinrich Himmler, the Nazi in charge of the camps, ordered all camps that could fall into Allied hands to be burned. Prisoners were to be evacuated by forced marches to more secure camps. Thousands died from exposure to the cold, starvation, disease, and planned slaughters along the way on these marches.

When the Allied forces entered the remaining camps in the spring of 1945, they came face to face with the true horror and scope of the Nazi atrocities. The dead and the living were found in piles together.

The sufferings of the Jews and other victims of Nazi persecution are known today as the "Holocaust." Although people shudder to remember it, most people agree that the world dare not forget that something as unthinkable as the Holocaust took place.

mountainous backbone of Italy, broke through Germany's defensive line at Monte Cassino in May 1944, and pushed toward Rome. The Allies marched into Rome on June 4, 1944, then continued to push the Germans out of Italy. Fascist Italy had fallen, and Hitler's armies were in retreat everywhere. It was time for the death blow to Germany—the Allied invasion of Normandy in France.

THE LAST DAYS OF HITLER

In December 1943 Roosevelt and Churchill met with Stalin for the first time to plan the cross-channel invasion for the spring of 1944. Stalin agreed to mount an attack along the eastern front at the same time. Finally—after a delay caused by bad weather—5,000 ships carrying 156,000 men left England to cross the English Channel. Eisenhower started the operation with the simple phrase "OK, let's go."

Operation Overlord was a complex invasion involving assaults on five separate Normandy beaches (see the map), parachute and glider landings, and air attacks. The Allied attack took the Germans completely by surprise— they had expected an attack much farther east at Calais. Nevertheless, the Allied forces had to fight many stiff battles, especially on the beach they called "Omaha" and at the city of Caen.

Once the beachhead was secure, the Allies advanced quickly

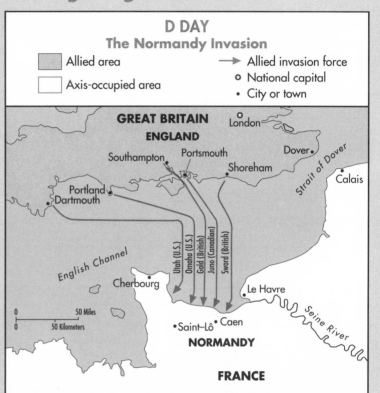

Operation Overlord: The Beginning of the End

D DAY
The Normandy Invasion

Allied area
Axis-occupied area
→ Allied invasion force
⊕ National capital
• City or town

The invasion of Normandy—called D day—was launched on June 6, a day later than planned. Heavy rains had held the Allies back, but Eisenhower finally ordered the assault.

The Allies had to crack heavy fortifications that the Germans had built in northern France— "Fortress Europe," Hitler called it. The U.S. Army was assigned two locations to attack (see map), as were the British. Canadians stormed a fifth beach. The Germans were surprised; they expected the attack farther east, near Calais.

After breaking through the German defenses, the Allies poured in equipment and more troops (see photograph). It was the beginning of the end for the Third Reich.

through France. On August 24, 1944, the French could celebrate. That day U.S. troops led by Free French troops under General Charles de Gaulle swept into Paris, to the cheers of the French people.

Hitler still had a few surprises of his own, however. In June 1944 he began air attacks on Britain, using V-1 buzz bombs and V-2 rocket bombs to create terror. Although there were over 50,000 British casualties and 75,000 homes destroyed, the scare tactic did not affect the Allied advance into Germany.

Hitler's second surprise was a concentrated attack on the 1,000-mile Allied front along the Ardennes plateau in northeastern France and southern Belgium. German troops punched a 50-mile hole in the front. The Allies destroyed much of the German

Eisenhower and MacArthur: Soldiers of Destiny

Two great American generals dominated military operations during World War II. One, Dwight D. Eisenhower (1890–1969), used diplomacy and a personal approach to unite the Allies' multinational forces and lead them to victory in Europe. The other, Douglas MacArthur (1880–1964), was the colorful and often controversial commander of the U.S. Army in the Pacific.

Both men were West Point graduates, and Eisenhower served as assistant to MacArthur when the latter was chief of staff of the Army and military adviser to the Philippines (1933–1939). Eisenhower described his senior officer as forceful, sometimes overpowering, and politically well-informed. He also said that MacArthur had a photographic memory and a vast store of knowledge. Always a showman with a big ego, MacArthur knew how to project a public image. He inspired many Americans early in the war when—after being ordered to leave the Philippines—he pledged, "I shall return." MacArthur made good on this famous resolve in 1944, when he waded ashore with the U.S. troops that had just landed to retake the Philippines.

▼ ▼ ▼

"*People of Western Europe: A landing was made this morning on the coast of France by troops of the Allied Expeditionary Force. . . . I call upon all who love freedom to stand with us now.*"

—Eisenhower, on D day

Eisenhower was a much different man and leader. Easygoing and likable, he spent the first part of his military career writing about and analyzing America's military strength. By the time of the bombing of Pearl Harbor, he had not yet been tested as a commander in battle. Yet he was appointed the commander of the U.S. forces in Europe (1942) and then the Allied supreme commander for the invasion of Europe (1943).

Eisenhower proved to be a superb strategist with an outstanding ability to coordinate the talents of others. Known to everyone as "Ike," he inspired confidence and became one of the most popular personalities of the war years. It was said that Eisenhower's "smile was worth 20 divisions."

One of the general's most brilliant and successful moves was to create a joint command headquarters, joining a British officer with an American officer in each position. He never lost sight of the importance of the human element in war. "Morale," he once wrote, "is supreme on the battlefield."

army in this brutal Battle of the Bulge (December 1944–January 1945). The victory ended Hitler's last effort to keep the Allies off German soil.

On the eastern front, the Soviets launched a massive offensive in 1944, which became the "Year of Ten Victories." The Soviet army liberated the Ukraine and then pushed on into Poland and Romania. The Crimean peninsula "turned red with blood" as the Soviets crushed the Nazis and recaptured Sevastopol. When the Soviets advanced to the Balkan countries, these old Axis allies rushed to switch sides. By January 1945, Stalin had penetrated deep into German territory with his own blitzkrieg—1.2 million Soviet troops supported by 6,000 airplanes.

At the Yalta Conference, held in February of 1945, Roosevelt, Churchill, and Stalin drew up terms for the postwar settlement. Europe would be divided into "spheres of influence," and Germany was to be disarmed, partitioned, and made to pay war damages. The Big Three powers would jointly occupy Berlin. By the time of the final Allied wartime conference at Potsdam (July–August 1945), Stalin held the position of strength. Roosevelt had died and been replaced by Truman; Churchill was to be replaced soon by Clement Atlee. The three leaders confirmed the Yalta agreement but endlessly debated without deciding the shape of the postwar world. In reality, however, the Cold War between the Soviet Union and the West had begun. The Soviet Union occupied the Balkans and

annexed much of East Prussia, part of Finland, and other neighboring territories. Stalin had made his intentions clear in a 1944 speech, saying: "Everyone imposes his own systems as far as his army can reach."

On April 30, 1945, as the Soviet army burned down the Reichstag in Berlin, Hitler realized that defeat was at hand and shot himself. On May 7, 1945, Germany signed the unconditional surrender that ended World War II in Europe. May 8 was proclaimed Victory in Europe (VE) day, and the people of the West celebrated.

World War II claimed the lives of 15 million to 20 million troops (7.5 million of them Soviet troops) and 25 million civilians (10 million of them Soviet citizens). Much of Europe was left in shambles, and the United States and the Soviet Union emerged as the major world powers. Distrust, suspicion, and fear would shape future relations between these two countries because of their conflicting goals and political systems.

▲ This scene of destruction in the industrial Ruhr valley of Germany was common throughout that country by 1945. Intense Allied bombing of Germany's cities far surpassed the Blitz of England earlier in the war.

GERMANS LEAD THE WAY IN GUIDED MISSILE TECHNOLOGY

The V-1 missile was a low-flying rocket that carried a high-explosive warhead. Although the guidance system for the V-1 was extremely crude by today's standards, it was effective enough to direct missiles from German-held countries in Western Europe to cities in England.

The V-2 was the first rocket-powered ballistic missile. Most V-2s contained a guiding device that cut off the rocket's fuel supply at the precise moment it was to descend on its target. Today's intercontinental ballistic missiles (ICBMs) use an advanced version of the same guiding device.

THE WAR IN THE PACIFIC

As early as 1933 President Roosevelt, at his first Cabinet meeting, warned that America could be forced into a war with Japan. In 1937 Japan launched a full-scale invasion of China, and within months controlled China's coastline, major cities, and most rail lines. Roosevelt began strengthening U.S. defenses in the Pacific.

By 1940 the Japanese had become even more aggressive under the leadership of War Minister General Hideki Tojo, who became prime minister in 1941. After Japan invaded French Indochina and signed a friendly three-way agreement with Italy and Germany, Roosevelt banned U.S. oil and iron exports to Japan. In 1941 he sus-

▼ Japan's empire reached its greatest extent in 1942. It held much of China and Southeast Asia as well as hundreds of Pacific islands. Japanese forces threatened Australia; the Allied victory at the Coral Sea helped turn the tide.

pended all finance and trade and froze Japanese assets in the United States. Britain and the Netherlands (the other major colonial powers in Asia) followed suit. Japan was now cut off from vital supplies. Confrontation with the West was inevitable.

Japan's overall goal was to form an Asian sphere of influence by "liberating" the colonies of East Asia from their Western "overlords," thereby keeping "Asia for the Asiatics." Japan's great naval strategist, Admiral Yamamoto, decided that the first blow in his country's contest with the West should be a strong one. He planned to destroy U.S. power in the Pacific while attacking British and Dutch territories in Asia.

At dawn on December 7, 1941, the plan was executed with deadly precision as Japan staged a surprise bombing attack on the U.S. Pacific Fleet at Pearl Harbor. The United States lost 18 ships destroyed or damaged beyond repair, 188 planes destroyed, and about 2,400 men and women killed. (See the feature in The Nation.) The only good news for the U.S. Navy was that its three aircraft carriers were not at the base and so were undamaged. Elsewhere, the Japanese bombed the British in Singapore and U.S. airfields in the Philippines and on Guam, Wake, and Midway islands. They landed troops in Malaya and Thailand. On December 8, the United States and Britain declared war on Japan.

The Allies on the Defensive

Reeling from Japan's successes and not fully prepared for war, the

STORM CLOUD IN THE EAST
Japanese Expansion in the Pacific

◉ National capitals   • Cities

▢ Farthest reach of Japanese by 1942

USSR
OUTER MONGOLIA
MANCHURIA
KOREA   JAPAN
CHINA
Chungking
Tokyo
Hiroshima
Nagasaki
MIDWAY IS. (U.S.)
INDIA
OKINAWA   IWO JIMA
BURMA
PACIFIC OCEAN
FRENCH
THAILAND INDO-
CHINA
Philippine Sea
HAWAIIAN IS. (U.S.)
Manila
PHILIPPINES (U.S.)
MALAY STATES (Br.)
Singapore
NETHERLANDS INDIES
NEW GUINEA   GUADALCANAL
INDIAN OCEAN
Coral Sea
AUSTRALIA

Allies at first took a defensive position in the Pacific. By July 1942 Japan controlled all of eastern Asia and the western Pacific and was pushing toward India and the northern coast of Australia. The Japanese continuously bombed the Australian port of Darwin, important to Allied supply routes. Japanese submarines even entered Sydney harbor.

The fall of Malaya and Singapore (February 15, 1942) was a humiliating defeat for the British army. In almost ten weeks the Japanese had destroyed Britain's air and sea power in Southeast Asia, captured the Malay peninsula, and bluffed the British into surrender at Singapore, even though the Japanese army there was outnumbered three to one. In April the last Allied troops in the Philippines surrendered. The Japanese seemed invincible.

In April 1942, the Allies had their first good news in the Pacific. Lieutenant Colonel James H. Doolittle led 16 B-25 bombers from the flight deck of the carrier *Hornet* on a bombing raid on Tokyo. All 16 planes made it safely to Japan.

The success of the mission heartened the Allies after so many defeats. It also had a more long-lasting effect. The surprised Japanese mistakenly believed that the attack had come from Midway Island and began planning an offensive there. Soon they would meet their doom.

The Allies soon had more good news: America scored a strategic victory in the Battle of the Coral Sea (May 1942). This effort kept Japan from cutting off Allied supply lines from Australia. It was the first sea battle in history in which two fleets fought without ever seeing each other: naval aircraft saw all the action.

The turning point in the Pacific war came at the Battle of Midway. Midway is a small atoll northwest of the Hawaiian islands. Hoping to destroy finally the U.S. Pacific Fleet, Yamamoto committed almost the

Major Events of the War in the Pacific

1931	Japan occupies Manchuria
1937	Japan invades China
Dec. 7, 1941	Japan attacks Pearl Harbor
Feb. 15, 1942	Singapore falls to Japan
April 9, 1942	U.S. and Philippine troops surrender at Bataan
April 18, 1942	Doolittle's raid on Tokyo
May 4–8, 1942	Battle of the Coral Sea
June 4–6, 1942	Battle of Midway
Aug. 7, 1942–Feb. 1943	Battle of Guadalcanal
Nov. 24, 1943	U.S. invades Gilbert Islands
Feb. 1–22, 1944	U.S. invades Marshall Islands
June 19–20, 1944	First Battle of the Philippine Sea
July 8, 1944	Tojo resigns
Oct. 23–26, 1944	Battle of Leyte Gulf; kamikazes first used
Oct. 20, 1944	U.S. invades Philippines at Leyte
Nov. 1944	U.S. begins bombing raids on Japan
Feb. 23, 1945	U.S. liberates Manila
Feb. 19–March 17, 1945	Battle of Iwo Jima
April 1–June 29, 1945	Battle of Okinawa
April 12, 1945	FDR dies; Truman becomes president
May 1945	Allies retake Burma
Aug. 5, 1945	A-bomb dropped on Hiroshima
Aug. 7, 1945	A-bomb dropped on Nagasaki
Aug. 8, 1945	Soviet Union declares war on Japan
Aug. 14, 1945	Japan surrenders unconditionally

entire Japanese navy to an attack. Because American intelligence had broken the Japanese military code, Admiral Nimitz, commander of the U.S. Pacific Fleet, had time to get ready. Nimitz decided to employ the long-range striking ability of his aircraft carriers instead of sending out battleships. American Navy pilots went to meet Yamamoto's fleet and succeeded in destroying Japan's main naval force.

Island Hopping

After the victory at Midway, the Allies began the difficult task of recapturing the Pacific islands from Japan. Their offensive began with the bloody six-month battle at Guadalcanal in the Solomon Islands (August 1942–January 1943). American Marines endured heat, humidity, swarms of biting insects, and tropical diseases as they dug in. Their mission was to hold the island against the constant stream of Japanese reinforcements, which arrived nightly by sea on what was called the "Tokyo Express." The Americans were finally victorious.

In March 1943 the Allies launched two thrusts toward Japan: General MacArthur's forces pushed through the southwest Pacific islands while Admiral Nimitz's fleet moved from island to island across the central Pacific. The Allied victory in the Battle of the Bismarck Sea (located between the islands of New Britain and New Guinea) spelled doom for Japan's power in the Pacific.

The Allies fought the biggest aircraft carrier battle of the war—the Battle of the Philippine Sea—en route to the Mariana Islands. American aircraft shot down so many Japanese planes in the 1944 battle for the Marianas that U.S. pilots called it the "Great Marianas Turkey Shoot." With the capture of the Marianas, the Allies were close enough for bombers to strike at Japan itself.

Meanwhile MacArthur led U.S. Army troops back to the Philippines in October 1944. He recaptured the islands after Japan's naval power was destroyed for good in the three-day battle of Leyte Gulf. During this naval battle, Japan began to use kamikaze attacks. Rather than dropping bombs, suicide pilots crashed their

▼ U.S. Marines raise a flag of victory near the end of the battle for Iwo Jima. The War Department was pleased when photographers could send these images of triumph back to the people at home.

planes into U.S. ships, causing great damage.

Iwo Jima and Okinawa

In February 1945 after 74 days of bombing and 3 days of naval bombardment on the island of Iwo Jima, 30,000 Marines landed to find that the Japanese had hidden in caves, tunnels, and bombproof underground hideouts. The fight for Iwo Jima became the bloodiest operation in U.S. Marine Corps history. As Marines crawled over the island, unseen Japanese cut them down. Finally the Marines captured the airfields and raised the American flag on top of the island's volcanic mountain. But the Japanese staged one last suicidal charge, leaving 800 Americans dead. When the battle was over, the Marines had lost 6,821 men, with 18,000 wounded.

At Okinawa, the Japanese staged ten massed kamikaze attacks that almost destroyed the Allies' Pacific Fleet. Japan sacrificed 1,465 aircraft and their pilots, but only managed to sink 11 Allied ships and damage 102 more. On land the Allies fought a strong Japanese resistance before winning the island. Now America was ready to deliver the final blow.

The Birth of the Atomic Age

On the morning of August 6, 1945, a 4-ton atomic bomb named "Little Boy" was dropped from a U.S. bomber onto the Japanese city of Hiroshima. The city became an instant wasteland and a burning grave for almost 100,000 people. Thousands of people were killed instantly, shock waves flattened

▲ The mushroom cloud from the atomic bomb dropped on Nagasaki was the symbol of a new era. President Truman and his advisers feared high American casualties if an invasion of Japan was necessary to end the war. They chose to drop two atomic bombs to end the fighting sooner.

buildings, and black raindrops began to fall as a mushroom-shaped cloud rose above the fireball. The bomb soon claimed another 100,000 victims as deadly radiation poisoning spread silently over the city and surrounding area.

When Japan still did not surrender, a second atomic bomb, called "Fat Man," was dropped onto Nagasaki on August 9. Again, much of the city was wiped out and thousands died. The shock of the second attack convinced Japan to surrender. Britons and Americans celebrated Victory in Japan (VJ) day on August 14. The formal Japanese surrender came on board the U.S.S. *Missouri* on September 2, 1945.

World War II was officially over, but the world had been changed forever. It had entered the atomic age. It had also entered a new phase, with the United States and the USSR emerging as superpowers. The shadow of the mushroom cloud made future contests between the two political giants doubly tense and frightening.

"Sixteen hours ago an American airplane dropped one bomb on Hiroshima . . . [with] more power than 20,000 tons of TNT. It is an atomic bomb. . . . If they do not now accept our terms, they may expect a rain of ruin from the sky the likes of which has never been seen on this earth."

—Harry S. Truman, 1945

BUSINESS AND ECONOMY

The Great Depression brought tremendous hardship to millions of Americans. Men who once held steady jobs were forced to eke out a living. Some took such desperate steps as selling sandwiches for 3 cents each, as the photograph shows. Such scenes were common. Unemployment ranged from 15 to 25 percent of the workforce throughout the decade. Even in 1939, 17 percent of workers were without jobs.

With one-sixth to one-quarter of all workers unemployed, the Depression touched all parts of the country and every level of society. Most people came to blame business and financial leaders for the crisis. President

AT A GLANCE

▶ The Great Depression

▶ Agriculture and the New Deal

▶ The Bank Crisis

▶ Labor Versus Management

▶ The Wartime Economy

Roosevelt's New Deal policies helped people cope with their hardships and improved the economy somewhat. Full recovery did not take effect until the war started in Europe, however. Then the need for war materiel fueled a boom.

Depression-era legislation left an enduring mark on the American economic system. For the first time the federal government took an active role in shaping and regulating the economy, controlling certain business and banking practices, and providing direct help to citizens in need. Many of these measures have become a fundamental part of the American social and economic scene.

DATAFILE

Wealth and productivity	1930	1945
Gross national product	$90.4 bil.	$211.9 bil.
Per-capita income	$625.00	$1,223.00
Trade balance		
Imports	$4.4 bil.	$10.2 bil.
Exports	$5.4 bil.	$16.3 bil.
Dow-Jones average	294.07	195.82
Raw steel output (short tons)	44.6 mil.	79.7 mil.
Auto factory sales	2.8 mil.	69,500

Labor force	1930	1945
Total	48.8 mil.	65.3 mil.
Male	78.1%	70.8%
Female	21.9%	29.2%
Unemployment rate	8.9%	1.9%
Union membership	3.6 mil.	14.8 mil.

Government	1930	1945
Federal spending	$3.1 bil.	$95.2 bil.
National debt (–) or surplus (+)	+$900.0 mil.	–$45.0 bil.

MARKET BASKET
Retail Prices of Selected Items, 1937

 Bread (1 lb.): **$0.09**

 Three-minute phone call (New York to Denver): **$4.50**

 Milk (½ gal., delivered): **$0.25**

 Car (Cadillac LaSalle V-8): **$1,095.00**

 Woman's dress: **$16.95**

 Movie ticket: **$0.15**

 Man's suit: **$40.00**

 Record player: **$189.50**

 Postage (1st class, 1 oz.): **$0.03**

 Electricity (per kilowatt hour): **$0.02**

THE GREAT DEPRESSION

When the stock market crashed, *Variety*—the trade magazine for show business—proclaimed the news as if a new Broadway show had flopped: WALL ST. LAYS AN EGG. The crash, though dramatic, did not cause the Great Depression. That slow, severe economic collapse started in mid-1929 when purchasing declined and construction dropped. Behind the outward prosperity of the mid-1920s, some destructive conditions were eating away at the nation's economic health. True, the stock market and real estate were booming, and a few industries, including the auto industry, recorded high profits. But many more industries, such as coal, railroads, and textiles, had slow growth and weak profits. Farmers were already in an economic depression; their decline in purchasing power was felt throughout the country.

The unequal distribution of income added to the problem. The wealthy, who could afford to buy many goods, were few in number. At the other end of the scale were millions of poor people who could afford to buy little. The people in the middle were not numerous enough to purchase all the excess goods. As a result, the supply of goods exceeded demand. The situation grew worse in 1930 when the Hoover administration placed high import taxes on foreign goods. Other countries responded by increasing their tariffs on American exports. This step lowered the demand for U.S. goods even more.

HELP WANTED

In 1931 the Soviet Union advertised in the United States for skilled workers. Over 100,000 Americans turned in applications, though there were only 6,000 jobs.

The rise in the use of credit in the 1920s seemed to be a sign of economic health. Increased credit often signals growth because businesses borrow money in order to expand. Most of the new borrowing in the 1920s, however, was by low-paid workers. Thus, the expanding credit system was on shaky ground. If those workers lost their jobs, they would be unable to repay the loans. That, in turn, would hurt banks and finance companies.

In 1929 the economic house of cards began to fall. Spring of that year brought a major drop in new construction. A rapid decline in stock prices followed in the fall and brought the stock market crashing down. Since the mid-1920s, the big money players on Wall Street had been on a stock-buying spree fueled by **speculation**. Loans were used to fund many of these stock purchases. When the lenders asked to be repaid, investors did not have enough cash on hand. They were forced to sell stocks to pay off the loans. The buying spree turned into a selling frenzy.

"Brother, Can You Spare a Dime?"

By 1931 more than 8 million people were unemployed, with more than 40 million living hand-to-mouth. Desperate for work, men would walk city streets carrying signs advertising their qualifications or make the rounds of employment agencies. Agencies would average 5,000 applicants a day for fewer than 200 job openings. Some jobless even paid a fee to get a temporary job. A man who bought work might pay $10 for a job that would pay only $13.50—but with the extra $3.50 he could then feed his family. Ragged bands of homeless youths, victims of broken families, roamed city streets and the countryside begging or stealing and sleeping in "hobo jungles." In the cities, hungry people would pick through garbage cans for food scraps, while in rural America many people stayed alive by eating wild berries, weeds, and flowers.

▼ ▼ ▼

"Once I built a railroad,
made it run,

Made it race against time.

Once I built a railroad,

Now it's done

Brother, can you spare a dime?"
—Depression era song

The most visible sign of the Depression was the breadline. Run by local charities and private groups, thousands of these breadlines operated in towns and cities across the country. People would wait in line for hours. Their clothing was threadbare, often lined with newspaper for warmth, their shoes stuffed with cardboard to cover holes. Reporter Bruce Bliven of the *New Republic* described a 1930 breadline in New York City: "There is a line of men, three or sometimes four abreast, a block long, and wedged together tightly. . . . For this compactness there is a reason: those at the head of this grey-black human snake will eat tonight; those farther back probably won't."

While conditions had improved by mid-decade, Roosevelt's 1936 inaugural address acknowledged that work remained to be done. He said that one-third of the population lacked adequate food, clothing, and shelter.

Effects of the Depression

From 1930 to 1939 Americans endured the most devastating economic crisis in their history. In those years poverty became a way of life for 40 million people. Hungry, jobless, and often homeless, people struggled to stay alive. The national income, which had been $87 billion in 1929, dropped by more than half to $40 billion by 1933, the worst year of the Depression. The nation's wealth declined by a quarter, from $439 billion prior to the crash to $330 billion in 1933. Between 1930 and 1933, 86,000 businesses failed.

On the individual level, wages fell 60 percent. In 1929 an executive secretary in New York City was making $45 per week; by 1932 he or she earned only $16 weekly. Local governments were unable to pay public employees because bankrupt individuals could no longer pay property taxes. As a result, garbage lay uncollected in the streets.

The banking industry was teetering on the brink of collapse, and constant rumors of new bank failures sent depositors scurrying to retrieve their money. Some banks closed their doors without warning during the middle of the day, leaving customers stunned. By 1933, 11,000 banks had failed. With these failures, the jobless lost their cushion against hard times: 9 million savings accounts were wiped out. Many states declared "bank holidays." They suspended banking operations to forestall further panic.

Other businesses and industries dealt with the economic crisis with varying degrees of success.

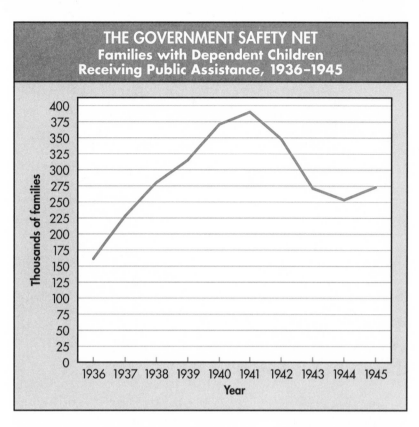

THE GOVERNMENT SAFETY NET
Families with Dependent Children Receiving Public Assistance, 1936–1945

Some survived and even showed modest growth by reducing their workforces, lowering wages, and cutting back to a five-day workweek. Other companies could not maintain operations and simply went bankrupt. At the end of the decade most businesses that survived were showing a profit. The war years would put American industry on top again, bringing unprecedented growth, profit, and respect for its contribution to the war effort.

The slowdown in construction that started in early 1929 was not completely obvious. Some major projects had already been started, and work continued during the decade. New York City alone saw four major projects. The Empire State Building and the Waldorf-Astoria Hotel were both completed in 1931. The George Washington Bridge was finished during the

▲ The Depression kept a firm grip on the economy for the entire decade. Note that the number of families receiving aid more than doubled between 1936 and 1940.

▲ The British Empire Building (foreground) and the 70-story RCA tower (background) were but two parts of the 14-building Rockefeller Center.

WORKERS BENEFIT
On June 25, 1938, President Franklin D. Roosevelt signed the Fair Labor Standards bill. The resulting law, which applied to workers in interstate commerce, set the minimum wage at 25 cents an hour and established a 44-hour workweek. In addition, the law ensured time-and-a-half pay for overtime work. It also prohibited wage discrimination based on age or sex. Finally, the law forbade employers to hire workers younger than 16 years of age.

Depression, and the huge Rockefeller Center complex of office buildings and retail space was constructed between 1931 and 1937. However, these few projects were not enough to keep the construction industry from suffering a severe slump.

While 1933 was the worst year of the Great Depression, effects of the crisis were still evident at the end of the decade. Some economic improvement occurred under President Roosevelt's New Deal, but a **recession** in 1937 and 1938 showed just how fragile the economy still was.

Economic Experimentation

When Roosevelt became president in March 1933, he had no tried-and-true formula for dealing with the Depression. Instead, the key words of his economic strategy, known as the New Deal, became *act* and *experiment*. Try something, he told his advisers—*anything*. If one program proved not to work, Roosevelt would try another program. The result was a patchwork of laws and federal agencies to carry out their provisions. Some programs were meant to be temporary, such as the Civil Works Administration. Others were reworked and changed over the years. Most aspects of the Public Works Administration, for instance, were absorbed into the Works Progress Administration. Many enjoyed wide popularity among the suffering populace. Both the National Recovery Administration and the Civilian Conservation Corps had broad public support. Some—like the NRA—were voided by the Supreme Court.

Overall, Roosevelt's New Deal policies were designed to provide aid for people in need and to stimulate business and consumer demand for goods. To one degree or another, they reached their desired goals; they also brought along some unplanned side effects, namely more and lasting government control of business and the whole economy.

During the first New Deal, Roosevelt tried to stimulate the economy by reviving industry and trade. To that end, he promoted cooperation and fair competition among business owners, backed higher wages for workers, and tried to level off the production and pricing of goods. Roosevelt switched his approach during the second New Deal, choosing to stimulate the economy directly by paying people to work on public works projects.

The most controversial legislation of the early New Deal was the National Industrial Recovery Act

(1933), which created the National Recovery Administration (NRA). The law gave the president the power to set codes for industries to ensure fair competition and labor practices. The NRA's purpose was to spread employment, set minimum wages, and stabilize prices. But doubts about its constitutionality arose immediately, and strong opposition came from business. The Supreme Court declared the NRA **unconstitutional** in 1935. A number of its main features reappeared in later New Deal laws.

Economic Innovations

Three New Deal programs introduced in 1933 not only were innovative but also had long-lasting economic effects. First was a three-pronged effort to help farmers. The Farm Credit Administration was established by executive order to handle all federal agencies that dealt with farm credit. Then two laws helped get needed money to farmers. The first permitted the Farm Credit Administration to sell bonds and use the money to help farmers refinance loans. The second allowed the government to lend money directly to farmers.

The second innovation was Roosevelt's brainchild, the Civilian Conservation Corps (CCC). The CCC provided jobs for young men between the ages of 17 and 25 who lived in cities. They began to restore national historic sites, build national park facilities, fight forest fires, and assist with drought relief. During its nine-year existence, the CCC employed about 3 million men, who planted over 2 billion trees, earning the workers the nickname "Roosevelt's Tree Army."

Members of the CCC were organized into groups of 200 and boarded in work camps. Their pay amounted to a dollar a day. They were required to send most of their earnings to help their families. The CCC also provided education; about 35,000 men learned to read and write while serving in the corps. The CCC helped preserve, protect, and improve the environment. At the same time it provided needed jobs. By late 1932 more than 25 percent of single men between the ages of 15 and 24 were unemployed. Another 29 percent were only working part-time. By 1935 over 500,000 of these young men were working in over 2,500 CCC camps across the country.

The third innovative early New Deal program grew out of public and congressional requests voiced by 1933. People were calling on the federal government to increase its spending and thereby stimulate the economy. Roosevelt responded by creating the Public Works Administration (PWA). Under the PWA, government funds provided jobs and money for constructing

HENRY AGARD WALLACE

Henry Wallace is probably most famous for serving as President Franklin D. Roosevelt's vice president from 1940 to 1944. However, his work as a plant geneticist is also notable.

Wallace began his career as a newspaper reporter and editor. During the mid-1920s, he also performed genetic research and eventually developed the first high-yield hybrid corn.

Wallace was appointed secretary of agriculture by Franklin D. Roosevelt in 1933. In this position, Wallace supervised New Deal programs that provided assistance for struggling farmers. As vice president during Roosevelt's third term, Wallace was an outspoken defender of liberal causes.

▼ The WPA, created in 1935, did more than fund building projects. These Vermont WPA workers were canning, one of scores of different programs established by the agency.

roads, tunnels, dams, bridges, and water and sewage systems.

Although it did not bring economic recovery, the PWA introduced a new practice. The federal government gave money directly to local governments. PWA projects also introduced a federal housing program. Many PWA public works, such as the Lincoln Tunnel between New York City and New Jersey, are still in use. Perhaps even more important, the PWA paved the way for the Works Progress Administration (WPA), created in 1935 to provide relief for the unemployed on a much broader scale.

The WPA went beyond building and construction projects. It also provided special programs that employed artists, musicians, writers, and actors. These programs—the Federal Writers' Project and Federal Theatre Project—were truly innovative. Their WPA workers wrote guidebooks or performed plays in rural towns. By the begin-

ning of World War II, more than 8 million people had held jobs with the WPA. The program had built more than 2,500 new hospitals, 5,900 schools, and thousands of public parks and utility plants.

In general, Roosevelt emphasized practical and speedy measures throughout the New Deal. He never backed off from changing direction or taking risks. At times he was inconsistent. He would cut government spending to hold down prices on the one hand, yet start huge programs like the WPA, which tend to create **inflation.** His programs provided relief for many jobless people and started the economy moving. Despite the New Deal's many successes, however, at the end of the decade recovery was far from complete.

AGRICULTURE AND THE NEW DEAL

Farmers were desperate. Many farmers burned corn for fuel or let crops rot in the fields because it would not pay to harvest them. Thus, while thousands of jobless people were roaming the country looking for food and work, tons of food was rotting in fields or being purposely destroyed. Farmers had seen rough times during the 1920s. The economic crisis of the 1930s—combined with natural disasters—worsened their situation.

Trouble on the Farm
The farmers' mood turned hostile. Some farmers protested by setting

▼ This Pennsylvanian and his family take the news hard: the bank has taken possession of their farm because they failed to make mortgage payments.

up roadblocks to keep goods from getting to market and by dumping milk along roadsides. Sometimes the unrest erupted into violence. In several counties in Iowa, military control had to be imposed to restore order.

Farmers who could not meet mortgage payments lost their homes to the banks. These banks frequently held public auctions to sell the farms. Other farmers would gather at these sales carrying pitchforks, clubs, and shotguns to scare off any outsiders who might try to bid on a neighbor's farm. Then they would take over the bidding and buy the livestock, equipment, and the land at very cheap prices. In the end, they returned the farm to its original owner.

Nature also conspired against farmers. A prolonged drought across the Great Plains began in 1933. After weeks without rain, winds whipped the topsoil into huge, black, destructive clouds of dust that swirled across the country. A series of devastating dust storms caused Midwesterners to refer to the period as the "dirty thirties"; layers of dust coated everything. The worst year for the Dust Bowl area was 1935, when the famous "black blizzard" of April 14 blew up. The storm piled dust like snow several feet high around buildings. Black clouds blocked the sun, plunging the area into long periods of total darkness.

Many farmers abandoned their once-fertile land and headed west looking for a better life. Between 1933 and 1938 almost 350,000 people from Kansas, Oklahoma, and Arkansas went to California only to find more hardship as mi-

DROUGHT ON THE PLAINS
The Dust Bowl, 1931–1938

⬜ Extent of the Dust Bowl

grant farm workers. The experiences of these "Okies" and "Arkies" were captured by John Steinbeck in his novel *The Grapes of Wrath*. The migration of farm families left many locations almost ghost towns. In Hall County, Texas, the population dropped by over 50 percent.

Regulation and Subsidies

Roosevelt planned to help farmers by dealing with the problems of overproduction and low prices first. Then he concentrated on getting new loans for farmers who needed equipment, setting up a program of soil conservation, and trying to help families who had left their land.

In 1933 the Agricultural Adjustment Administration (AAA) was established to increase farmers' income by regulating markets. It tried to create a balance between the prices the farmers received for their crops and the prices they

▲ The Dust Bowl covered a huge area, leaving thousands of acres destroyed and thousands of farmers hopeless.

THE GRAPES OF WRATH

One of the most powerful novels in American literature, John Steinbeck's *The Grapes of Wrath* (1939), tells the story of the Joads, a fictional Okie family. This excerpt describes what they found in California:

"He drove his old car into a town. He scoured the farms for work. Where can we sleep tonight?

"Well, there's Hoovervilles on the edge of the river. There's a whole raft of Okies there.

"He drove his old car to Hooverville. He never asked again, for there was a Hooverville on the edge of every town."

paid for manufactured goods. To that end, the government gave the farmers special payments called farm **subsidies** not to grow certain amounts of basic commodities, such as wheat, cotton, corn, and rice. The idea was to cut down on the amount of surplus food and thus raise prices.

Controversy arose over the AAA and its departure from traditional economic policy. In 1936 the Supreme Court declared part of the AAA unconstitutional. A year earlier the Court had also voided another act that had provided for a five-year delay against bank seizures of farms. Roosevelt was more successful in stopping the number of farm bankruptcies with a new version of the law passed in 1935. That act placed a three-year stoppage on farm seizures.

The Resettlement Administration (1935) helped many displaced

tenant farmers—a total of 4,441 families—to settle on new land. Further, it restored worn-out farmland through flood control and prevention of soil erosion. In 1937 these programs became part of the Farm Security Administration. That agency helped migrant workers by regulating wages and hours and aided tenant farmers by providing long-term loans to buy their own land.

Control of farm production was extended by the Soil Conservation and Domestic Allotment Act (1936). Under its provisions, farmers received subsidies for planting such soil-conserving crops as soybeans. The Agricultural Adjustment Act of 1938 proved partially successful in giving farmers a fair price for their crops and a larger share of the national income. It continued subsidies for farmers who limited the amount of land they planted.

Although many New Deal programs helped farmers, the farm economy remained fragile until World War II. Then demand for food used up surpluses and achieved a balance in prices.

▼ The prices of corn and wheat—two key crops—dropped and rose together. As New Deal farm price policies took hold in the late 1930s, those prices began a steady rise.

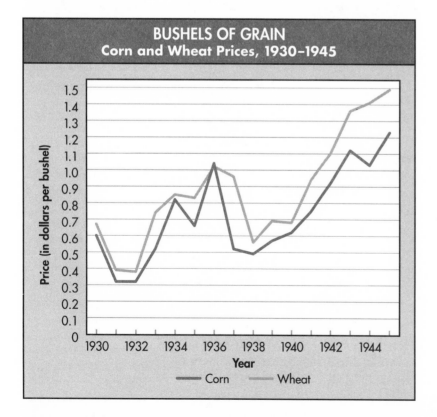

BUSHELS OF GRAIN
Corn and Wheat Prices, 1930–1945

Price (in dollars per bushel) vs Year

— Corn   — Wheat

Banking

THE BANK CRISIS

The country's banking system was near collapse in early 1933. As banks failed, panic-stricken people rushed to withdraw their money. With the intense demand for cash, more banks were forced out of business—which fed savers' panic even more. When Roosevelt took the oath of office on March 4, 1933, 38 governors had ordered all banks in their states closed in an attempt to halt the panic. A national solution was needed. The new president moved swiftly to introduce changes that would control abuses in the financial sector and restore people's confidence in the monetary system.

First he declared a nationwide week-long bank holiday. Banks were allowed to accept all deposits but withdrawals were banned. During that "holiday," Congress passed the Emergency Banking Relief Act, giving the president the power to regulate banking transactions and foreign exchange. To avoid panic, Roosevelt spoke on the radio, giving a reassuring "fireside chat." People responded by bartering (exchanging goods rather than purchasing them with money). For example, Madison Square Garden in New York City accepted such items as canned goods and shoes in exchange for prize-fight tickets. When the banks reopened—under government supervision—people no longer rushed to withdraw money, and some confidence was restored.

One of the most important steps in stabilizing the banking system came later in 1933. By forming the Federal Deposit Insurance Corporation (FDIC), the government insured deposits in all national and state banks in the Federal Reserve System. If a bank failed, depositors would no longer lose their money; the government would repay them. This promise gave people more security—and confidence. At first the FDIC insured deposits up to

$5,000; it now insures them up to $100,000.

In 1933 and 1934, Roosevelt took the country off the gold standard, the system of basing the value of paper money on the price of gold. He hoped that government purchase of gold at steadily rising prices would lower the value of the dollar, trigger a rise in wholesale prices, and stimulate foreign trade. By law, all gold had to be surrendered to the U.S. Treasury in exchange for paper currency. The government stopped buying gold in January 1934, and Congress enacted the Gold Reserve Act, which gave the president the power to fix the price of gold in the United States. Roosevelt eventually set that price at $35 an ounce. He also reduced the value of the dollar in the hope of forcing prices up, which would spur production.

Two other measures brought needed reforms in the financial system. First, the Truth-in-Securities Act of 1933 required stockbrokers to give their clients a complete and fair disclosure of all information about stocks, bonds, and other securities for sale. The aim here was to cut down on the sale of risky stocks and manipulation of stocks by brokers. Second, all interstate stock transactions had to be registered with the Federal Trade Commission. Finally, Congress created an independent agency, the Securities and Exchange Commission (SEC) in 1934. The SEC was given the job of policing the securities industry to prevent fraud and manipulation. Overall, New Deal laws succeeded in placing the banking and finance industries on stronger footing.

STFU PROTESTS UNFAIR EVICTIONS

The AAA's policies hurt many tenant farmers, who had no land but worked a landowner's fields and paid the landowner rent. According to the New Deal program, farmers were paid to let some of their land lie fallow (unplanted). Although they were supposed to split government payments with their tenants, many landowners kept the AAA money and evicted their tenants.

The Southern Tenant Farmers' Union (STFU) was founded to combat these unfair practices. By organizing strikes among tenant farmers and day laborers, the STFU won increases and a guarantee from the Department of Agriculture that they would receive their AAA payments.

The STFU was unusual because it was composed of black and white farmers who worked closely together.

MOTHER JONES

On November 30, 1930, Mary Harris Jones (known as "Mother Jones") died at the age of 100. Her death ended a 50-year career as a labor activist.

In 1867 Jones's husband and children died of yellow fever. A few years later, she lost all her possessions in the great Chicago fire. Once she began to attend weekly meetings of the Knights of Labor, she devoted herself to union work. Her idealism and energy carried her across the United States to speak out for laborers in cotton and steel mills, coal and copper mines, railroads, and the garment industry.

▼ Battles often broke out between strikers and the police, as shown here in a 1937 Chicago steel strike. Labor had the right to organize, but companies treated organizers harshly.

Labor

LABOR VERSUS MANAGEMENT

In March 1932 about 3,000 men marched on the Ford auto plant in Dearborn, Michigan, to demand jobs. Police pushed them back with guns and tear gas, resulting in four deaths and many wounded. At the funeral, workers carried banners reading, "Ford gave bullets for bread." Workers, desperate for help, found a friend in the White House.

The Roosevelt administration championed the workers' cause by creating federally funded jobs for the unemployed, establishing a minimum wage, ending unfair labor practices, and supporting the right to organize into unions. Early work relief efforts came with the creation of the Federal Emergency Relief Agency (1933), which gave $3 billion to states to use as wages on work projects or for payments to the unemployed. The Civil Works Administration (1933–1934) gave federal work relief to some 4 million people who built 469 airports and a number of other projects. New Deal agencies placed more than 11 million people in public work programs. Some people criticized these agencies, especially the CWA and WPA, saying that they sometimes created pointless, make-work jobs just to keep people off direct relief payments. These jobs were ridiculed as "boondoggling," and the WPA was laughingly renamed "We Piddle Around."

The government paid special attention to jobs for women in some of its programs. Ellen Sullivan Woodward became a powerful supporter of work for women. She served as assistant administrator of women's relief activities in three different agencies. She created a jobs program for women in every state and fought for equal pay for women.

Labor Declares War

Labor and management were ready for a showdown by the mid-1930s. Employment had risen and laws had given labor the right to unionize, but the companies still held all the power. Some hired men to beat or shoot anyone caught trying to unionize. The auto industry hired the Pinkerton Detective Agency to spy on workers. Auto companies paid a total of $1.75 million to identify which workers were actively seeking to unionize. If workers went on strike, companies called in strikebreakers who moved in to fill strikers' jobs.

A major labor-management battle came in 1934 when John L. Lewis, leader of the United Mine Workers of America (UMWA, usually "UMW"), called a strike in the Pennsylvania coal fields. Workers were being discouraged from joining the UMW. Widespread disorder and violence broke out, with mine owners bombing miners' homes. But in the end the UMW was accepted. Lewis turned to organize workers in other industries.

The American labor movement reached a milestone with the National Labor Relations Act in 1935. This act defined unfair labor practices, protected unions against company threats, and created the National Labor Relations Board. The board had the power to enforce the law. Labor marked another gain when Lewis founded the Committee for Industrial Organizations (CIO), a splinter group from the American Federation of Labor

"No tin-hat brigade of goose-stepping vigilantes or Bible-babbling mob of blackguarding corporation-scoundrels will prevent the onward march of labor."

—John L. Lewis, 1937

John L. Lewis: Union Organizer

John L. Lewis (1880–1969) introduced a new era of labor rights during the 1930s and early 1940s and became one of the most powerful men in the country. As president of the United Mine Workers of America (UMWA) from 1920 to 1960, he won many benefits for mine workers and helped increase union membership from 150,000 in 1930 to more than 600,000 by 1937. As a founder and first

president of the CIO, he unionized thousands of workers in such major industries as auto and steel. All his life, he championed the cause of labor.

Leaving school after the seventh grade, Lewis went to work in the coal mines of Iowa and Colorado. There he gained respect for his energy, labor views, and speaking ability. That ability came from his wide and close reading of such works as the Bible, the *Odyssey* and *Iliad,* and the works of Karl Marx and William Shakespeare. A tall, imposing man, Lewis was both a shrewd negotiator and a tough-minded leader who led several of the decade's major labor wars, from the coal miners' strikes in 1934 to the massive General Motors sit-down strike of 1936 and 1937. He also could use charm as a bargaining de-

vice. He got the chairman of the board of U.S. Steel to sign a pact with the CIO by talking of high finance and art.

Most of all, Lewis made the nation heed the call of labor through his eloquent speech. As he told the UMWA, "I have pleaded your cause not in the tones of a feeble mendicant asking for alms, but in the thundering voice of a captain of a mighty host, demanding the rights to which free men are entitled." By 1940 he had used his tremendous power to tear down many barriers to unions. He worked to establish health, welfare, and retirement funds and better wages and working conditions in many unionized industries. He helped to modernize mining by working with experts to introduce new machinery. He was a major figure of labor.

(AFL) in 1935. Lewis wanted to expand union membership to semi-skilled and unskilled workers, which the AFL did not include. He aimed to bring all workers in a particular industry into a single union. He targeted the huge auto and steel industries for union drives. The AFL leadership opposed this plan.

CIO Victories

During 1936 and 1937 labor activists staged a number of sit-down strikes and other actions against General Motors (GM) to gain the right to organize. After violent confrontations and the loss of $1 million a day in profits, GM gave in. Soon other automakers followed.

The UAW and the GM Sit-Down Strike

◁ Autoworkers celebrate victory in the 1937 GM sit-down strike.

As the strikes continued into January 1937, the situation became explosive, especially at a plant in Flint. GM turned off the heat in the plant, even though the outdoor temperature had dropped below zero. At GM's request, the police kept food from being sent in to the strikers. Protesters picketing outside were beaten with clubs, sprayed with tear gas, and peppered with buckshot. The strikers fought back with such weapons as pipes and coffee mugs; they eventually defeated the police in an all-night battle.

The crisis forced Michigan's governor to step in. He prohibited GM from denying food to the strikers. After 44 days of striking, GM gave in and agreed to accept the UAW. Chrysler and other auto companies also accepted the UAW that year. Ford held out until 1940.

In December 1936, 6,000 workers at General Motors' Cleveland plants laid down their tools and refused to work. They used this sit-down strike to win the right of the United Auto Workers (UAW) to bargain with GM. Thus began a war between GM, the third largest corporation in the country, and its workers. The bitter and often violent struggle ended with the acceptance of the UAW as the bargaining agent for almost the entire auto industry.

Tensions had been building among the autoworkers since GM had hired the Pinkerton Detective Agency to spy on its employees and prevent attempts to unionize. The workers chose the sit-down strike to halt production and prevent the hiring of strikebreakers.

Two days after the Cleveland workers began their strike, the men at GM's Chevrolet plant in Flint, Michigan, also staged a sit-down. Workers at 15 other GM plants did the same.

The United Auto Workers had won the right to bargain for workers throughout the auto industry.

Meanwhile Lewis was trying to unionize the steel industry. The industry giant, U.S. Steel, quickly signed an agreement with the CIO. But "Little Steel," smaller companies like Bethlehem Steel and Republic Steel, fought unionization. In May 1937 there began one of the bloodiest antiunion battles of the decade: 70,000 workers in seven states walked out of 27 plants belonging to "Little Steel." On Memorial Day about 2,000 protesters marched to the Republic Steel plant in South Chicago, where they were met with gas and bullets. The Memorial Day Massacre left 10 dead, more than 90 wounded, and broke the strike. Workers returned to work without a contract, but by 1941 all of "Little Steel" had signed contracts with the CIO.

Labor militancy calmed down after 1938, but the preceding years had seen many gains. Over 7 million workers belonged to unions. Workers had won contracts guaranteeing wages, hours, and safer working conditions. Lewis's CIO (renamed the Congress of Industrial Organizations) finally broke with the AFL in 1938, and by 1940 claimed 4 million members, including 200,000 blacks.

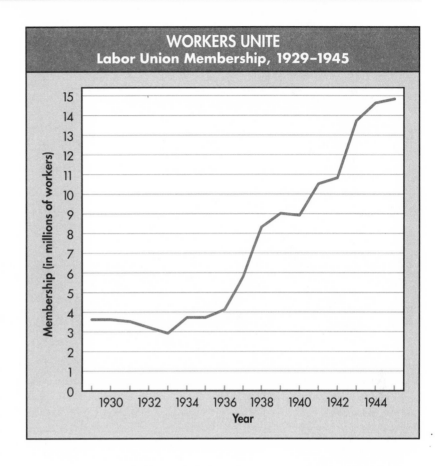

Union membership grew almost five times between 1930 and 1945. The big gain was from 1935 to 1937 as the CIO began to recruit industrial workers.

single war effort. Actually, Roosevelt had started preparing the nation for war as early as 1939. In 1940 he asked Americans to harness their resources and strengthen defenses to prepare for any emergency. He began a program of arms production and asked the aviation industry to produce 50,000 planes a year (compared to the 6,000 produced annually prior to 1940). Once Congress declared war, the government moved swiftly to transform the economy.

Economy

THE WARTIME ECONOMY

When America entered World War II on December 8, 1941, the entire country—its people and industries—had to be organized into a

The War Industry

Existing factories rapidly converted from peacetime to wartime production. The entire auto industry was transformed to mass-produce arms and military equipment. Within just 11 months the huge Chrysler Tank Arsenal had been

LABOR AND THE WAR EFFORT

Soon after Pearl Harbor, both the AFL and the CIO made no-strike promises. But strikes occasionally took place, and they damaged the public perception of unions. People saw these job actions—often over wages, not the right to unionize—as counter to the war effort. The overall number of work stoppages during the war, however, was much lower than that of the tumultuous 1930s.

▲ This photograph of International Harvester's Chicago plant shows the effects of wartime production: the plant produced both farm tractors for the home front and tractors ready to be sent to war in Europe or the Pacific.

built and began turning out General Grant tanks. Production reached over 25,500 tanks by 1945. Many companies whose products were unrelated to war industries obtained defense contracts to manufacture war materiel. For example, Coca-Cola operated a TNT plant.

Production figures for the war years are astounding. Industrial output almost doubled from 1939 to 1945. Fueling that growth were vast stores of weapons and supplies. Between July 1, 1940, and July 31, 1945, the American arms industry produced 71,000 naval ships, over 5,000 cargo ships, 200 submarines, almost 100,000 aircraft, 372,000 artillery pieces, 90,000 tanks, 20 million small arms, 41 billion ammunition rounds, and almost 6 million bombs. One reason output went up was the phenomenal increase in productivity. Shipbuilders were able to complete entire cargo ships

in 17 days. Aircraft workers reduced the time needed to make a bomber from 200,000 to 13,000 worker-hours. By 1944 the United States produced about 40 percent of the world's arms.

Some businesses cleverly capitalized on the special circumstances of a wartime economy. For example, Coca-Cola became the official soft drink of the U.S. armed forces. Wrigley's gained government permission to put three sticks of gum in every pack of emergency field rations for the troops.

"Rosie the Riveter"

The heroine of the home front was "Rosie the Riveter"—the proud, patriotic woman who went to work in an arms plant while her husband or boyfriend fought the war. While the image was meant to build morale, there was truth behind it. Women entered the workforce in record numbers during the war. Most of these women worked in traditionally female occupations, such as nursing, teaching, and clerical jobs. But many filled jobs that had previously been held by men only, such as work in aircraft plants, shipyards, and arms factories. They worked in swing shifts, riveting, welding, and assembling tanks, guns, and trucks.

In the early months of 1942, 750,000 women volunteered to work at armament plants. The number of women in the aircraft industry grew from 4,000 to 360,000. At least 40 percent of the workers at ammunition plants were women. By 1944, 3.5 million women were working in the defense industry along with 6 million male workers.

Price Controls and Rationing

With the production boom, earnings rose. Weekly earnings in manufacturing rose 70 percent. Low-paid workers and those who had been unemployed were suddenly making over $100 per week. Farmers started increasing production after years of federal subsidies to cut output. As a result, the net cash income of farmers climbed more than 400 percent from 1940 to 1945.

On the home front, employment and wages were up—and so was demand. Increased demand combined with war shortages of such items as meat, gas, and sugar caused prices to soar. To protect the consumer from unreasonable price hikes, Congress enacted the Emergency Price Control Act in January 1942. The law created the Office of Price Administration (OPA), which had authority to regulate prices and to establish a rationing program. The OPA froze commodity prices and the rents on houses and apartments near defense plants at their levels of March 1942.

Certain goods—gasoline, fuel oil, meat, sugar, and coffee—were in such demand for the armed forces that they became scarce on the home front. As a result, the OPA distributed ration books for those goods. Most Americans cooperated with the **rationing.** However, by the end of 1942 a black market existed for every item that was in short supply. During the height of the black market, people spent more than a million dollars a week to obtain illegal meat in Chicago.

Other items, such as cigarettes, nylon, rubber, and automobiles, remained scarce throughout the war. Production of cars for civilian use stopped in early 1942, and most new cars already off the assembly line were taken for military use. Americans kept the cars they had or bought used ones—if they could find them. By and large, consumer demand was kept pent up during all the war years. Consumers were ready to explode in a frenzy of buying once the war ended.

Financing the War

One way that people felt they could personally contribute to the war effort was by buying war bonds. Money from these bonds helped pay for war materials. The sale of war bonds also absorbed people's extra money, which helped prevent inflation. Large rallies were held in towns and cities across the nation to promote the buying of bonds. Celebrities like movie star Betty Grable, who auctioned her stockings, helped promote bond sales. Bond sales reached $135 billion.

To raise even more money Congress passed a revenue bill in 1942, which hiked corporate taxes and personal income taxes. Under the new law, 50 million people paid taxes, compared with only 13 million in 1941. Beginning in 1943, a new step in income taxes appeared. Businesses were directed to collect these taxes using payroll deductions. Despite these increased taxes, the huge cost of the war caused the total national debt to rise to $258 billion by the end of the war, almost six times what it was in 1941.

WARTIME RATIONING AFFECTS AMERICANS

The OPA's rationing plan worked this way: each person received ration stamps. When buying goods, shoppers had to present these stamps to the merchant, who in turn gave the stamps to suppliers in order to obtain more goods. It was not until the end of World War II that rationing ended and American consumers were allowed to purchase goods that had been scarce during the war.

SCIENCE AND TECHNOLOGY

The Depression and World War II each in its own way set the pace for advances in science and technology during the 1930s and early 1940s. As Americans struggled to rebuild the economy, funding for many scientific projects dwindled. By World War II, however, the federal government was pouring money into scientific research, particularly in atomic energy. New technological developments came as scientists and engineers worked to develop more effective weapons to help fight the war. Turning their new designs into actual guns, tanks, planes, and ships was the task of legions of workers such as those shown in the photograph above. Their efforts transformed the United States into the "arsenal of democracy."

AT A GLANCE

- ▶ The Power of the Atom
- ▶ The Dawn of the Age of Plastics
- ▶ Increasing Crop Yields During the Depression
- ▶ New Consumer Goods
- ▶ Breakthroughs in the Fight Against Disease
- ▶ Developments Made for War

Many important discoveries were made during this period. Sulfa drugs were discovered and used to fight bacterial infections. New materials, such as nylon and plastics, were developed. Research in agriculture led to disease-resistant crops and better methods of harvesting. Technological advances improved existing products such as the radio. Other innovations gave consumers new products, from the ballpoint pen to frozen foods.

The most far-reaching discoveries came from a better understanding of the atom. This new knowledge grew from decades of research and an intensive U.S. effort in a highly secret project. The results were the first atomic bomb and the birth of the atomic age.

DATAFILE

Science

Life expectancy at birth (yr.)

	1930	1945
Males	58.1	63.6
Females	61.6	67.9

Top five causes of death, 1930–1945
1. Heart and kidney diseases 2. Cancer
3. Influenza and pneumonia 4. Tuberculosis
5. Accidents (not including motor vehicle accidents or falls)

Technology

Miles of paved roads

1930 694,000   1945 1,721,000

Passenger miles traveled, 1945

Rail .... 91.8 bil.   Air .... 3.8 bil.

Tallest building in U.S., 1945

Empire State Building (completed 1931): New York City, 102 stories, 1,250 ft.

Households in 1940 with . . .

Electricity 78.7%
Telephone 36.9%
Indoor plumbing 61.5%

THE WILD BLUE YONDER
U.S. Production of Military Aircraft, 1939–1945

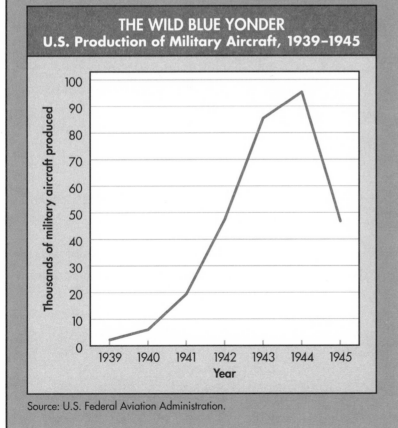

Source: U.S. Federal Aviation Administration.

THE POWER OF THE ATOM

Atomic physics—the study of the structure and behavior of atoms—had been an area of intense activity for decades. Scientists knew that atoms were made of particles called electrons and a nucleus at the atom's core. They believed that electrons revolved around that nucleus like planets around the sun. Scientists had also identified scores of elements, each differing in size and structure. The stage was set for more discoveries.

In 1932 the British physicist James Chadwick discovered that tiny, subatomic particles called "neutrons" help form the atom's nucleus. That year, an American physicist, Carl Anderson, identified another subatomic particle, the positron. Harold Urey, an American chemist, enlarged these insights by isolating deuterium, a heavy form of hydrogen. From these discoveries, scientists in Europe and America launched the modern age of nuclear research.

By 1934, a scientist named Leo Szilard had fled unrest in his native Hungary for London. Szilard theorized that the nuclei of certain atoms could be split if bombarded by neutrons. This splitting—later called **nuclear fission**—should release more neutrons. The process would then repeat itself in a chain reaction. In that year, Italian scientists led by Enrico Fermi did indeed use neutrons to split an atom of uranium. Fermi and his team did not realize that they had achieved fission, however. By late

1938 German scientists Otto Hahn and Fritz Strassman, who repeated the Italian experiment, recognized that fission had occurred.

The idea of a fission bomb had been on many minds for some time. German refugees Otto Frisch and Rudolf Peierls, working in Great Britain, demonstrated in 1939 that such a bomb was possible. Their secret was to split the atoms of a rare form of uranium called U-235. Another breakthrough came in 1941. By bombarding uranium with neutrons, scientists in California created an element heavier than uranium. Many scientists thought the element, called "plutonium," would work well for creating fission.

Fermi: Architect of Nuclear Power

An Italian-American physicist, Enrico Fermi (1901–1954), was one of the giants of atomic research. Many people regard him as the "father of the atomic age." In his early career Fermi helped establish modern physics in Italy and introduced the theory of monatomic gas (now called "Fermi gas"). This theory explained some properties of metals not understood before then.

In 1933 Fermi turned to nuclear research. He led a team in Rome that was the first to achieve nuclear fission of uranium, although he did not realize his momentous discovery at the time. His lifetime of nuclear research gained Fermi great fame, however. In 1938 he won the Nobel Prize in physics, with the award citing two achievements. Fermi was recognized first for producing a large number of radioactive isotopes through neutron bombardment. Fermi was noted also for his discovery that slow neutrons were very effective in producing radioactivity. These discoveries paved the way for the creation of the atomic bomb.

Fermi left Italy in 1938 because Fascist policies menaced his Jewish wife and threatened his freedom to work. He came to the United States in 1939 and became

▼ ▼ ▼

Many people regard him as the "father of the atomic age."

a citizen in 1944. Fermi continued his research into nuclear fission at Columbia University and the University of Chicago. Here, in 1942, he toiled in the squash court located under the stands of the university stadium. Fermi was not playing squash, though; he was building the world's first atomic reactor. When Fermi used that reactor to achieve the first sustained nuclear chain reaction in December 1942, the world entered the atomic age. From 1944 to 1945 he was associate director, under J. Robert Oppenheimer, of the Los Alamos, New Mexico, laboratories. In these positions, the two men helped design the first atomic bombs.

After the war Fermi became a professor at the University of Chicago's Institute for Nuclear Studies. To honor his work, that institute was renamed the Fermi Institute after his death. Fermi received other honors as well. In 1954 he received the first annual award of the U.S. Atomic Energy Commission. That award was given for outstanding achievement in the development, use, or control of nuclear energy. After his death, the award was named for him. In 1953 the American physicist Albert Ghiorso and his associates discovered a radioactive chemical element that they named "fermium" as a lasting tribute to Fermi.

As these discoveries were made, scientists in several countries asked their governments for money to do more fission research. By the late 1930s, Fermi and Szilard were living and working in the United States. Together with Albert Einstein, who had fled Germany earlier, they asked President Roosevelt to set up a program of nuclear research. The objective was to develop the bomb before German scientists did. Roosevelt agreed.

The Manhattan Project

In 1942 the largest and most secret single project in the history of science began in the United States. Its code name was the "Manhattan Project" because the initial work was done at Columbia University in New York City, in the Manhattan District of the U.S. Army Corps of Engineers. The project reached well beyond Manhattan, however. It eventually had 37 installations in the United States and Canada that employed 43,000 people. Security was so tight that many workers did not know the goal of the project. Scientists traveled under assumed names. Enrico Fermi's code name, for instance, was "Henry Farmer."

General Leslie Groves of the Army Corps of Engineers directed the project. J. Robert Oppenheimer ran the specially built complex at Los Alamos, New Mexico, where the bomb would actually be put together. Urey took charge of the effort to split U-235 in Oak Ridge, Tennessee. Arthur Compton coordinated research at universities on the East Coast, and Chadwick led a British team of scientists who also contributed.

◀ Oppenheimer (left) and General Groves stand near what remains of the steel tower that held the first atomic bomb. When detonated, the bomb melted the tower.

"The Shatterer of Worlds"

In 1942 Fermi used a nuclear reactor to achieve the first self-sustaining chain reaction. He succeeded in making plutonium. After that, members of the project focused on two separate methods to explode fission bombs, one for a uranium bomb and one for a plutonium bomb. Research wore on for months.

As the program continued, the decision was made to test the plutonium bomb. Work crews mounted it on a steel tower in the desert near Los Alamos. At dawn on July 16, 1945, it was detonated. In seconds, heat vaporized the tower and a gigantic fireball appeared. Then a mushroom-shaped cloud, which became the symbol of the atomic age, appeared and stretched 40,000 feet into the sky. Realizing the bomb's destructive potential, Oppenheimer quoted a line from the *Bhagavad Gita* (a Hindu religious text): "I am become death, the shatterer of worlds."

"It may be possible to set up a nuclear reaction in uranium by which vast amounts of power could be released. . . . This new phenomenon would also lead to the construction of . . . extremely powerful bombs of a new type."

—Albert Einstein, in a letter to President Roosevelt, 1939

Many scientists involved in the project now feared that an arms race would result, leading to the annihilation of mankind. They urged President Truman—in office since Roosevelt's death—not to use the bomb. Truman, however, saw the need to end the war and prevent further slaughter of U.S. soldiers in the Pacific. He decided to drop a bomb on a Japanese military site. Hiroshima was chosen because it had shipyards, industrial plants, and large military bases. On August 6, 1945, the uranium bomb, called "Little Boy," was dropped on that city from a B-29 bomber named *Enola Gay* (after the mother of the pilot).

On the following day, Truman informed the country of the event, pledging that Japan, if it did not surrender, "may expect a rain of ruin from the air, the like of which has never been seen on this earth." When Japan remained silent, the plutonium bomb, called "Fat Man," was dropped on Nagasaki on August 9. Japan quickly surrendered. The world had entered a new era.

PLASTIC PARTIES

The production of synthetic plastics in the United States skyrocketed during the Great Depression. U.S. production was 50 million pounds in 1930. By 1940 it was 250 million pounds.

Among these plastic products were the first Tupperware containers, invented in 1945. A Massachusetts chemist and inventor named Earl S. Tupper developed the line of polyethylene containers to be used as storage bowls in the kitchen. Tupper also devised a new way of marketing his products. He sold his storage bowls and boxes through in-home sales parties.

Plastics

THE DAWN OF THE AGE OF PLASTICS

What does a country do when war breaks out and it lacks raw materials? It uses substitutes. The United States, Great Britain, Germany, and other combatants faced this need. They built on years of progress in making **synthetic,** or human-made, materials. As a result, they had the needed substitutes. Plastics like polystyrene, polyvinyl chloride, polyethylene, and nylon were introduced and used in such items as drinking glasses, zippers, and hosiery. These plastics proved more versatile than the natural materials they replaced. They were also cheaper and more durable.

The German syndicate IG Farbenindustrie developed polystyrene, and the American company B. F. Goodrich invented polyvinyl chloride as early as 1930. An alternative to glass, polystyrene is clear, transparent, easily colored, and easy to make. It was used at first for such items as drinking glasses and containers. Polyvinyl chloride first went into use as a see-through coating that could protect a surface. Later, it became the raw material used for rain boots and upholstery. Other uses included phonograph records.

Two other plastics that date from this period are commonly used in the kitchen. Melamine formaldehyde, developed in 1935, was used to make high-quality dinnerware. Polyethylene, developed by the British company Imperial Chemical Industries in 1941, eventually went into the manufacture of such things as bags and food wraps. This product has also been used in wire insulation and a wide range of containers.

One of the most famous new materials of the time was nylon. Nylon first appeared in 1934, created by W. H. Carothers and his associates at the DuPont Company. Nylon came into full-scale production in 1938. First used in bristles for toothbrushes, nylon soon found widespread use in the hosiery industry. The new material proved much stronger than the natural silk fibers that had been used for stockings. By 1939, consumers had bought 64 million pairs of nylon stockings.

With further experimentation, nylon was found to be a general-purpose synthetic. By 1941, it had replaced natural substances in dozens of manufactured items for the home. It also appeared in waterproof umbrellas, shower curtains, and the strings of musical instruments and tennis rackets. Once the war broke out, nylon became an essential military material. It went into making protective vests for soldiers, parachutes, and reinforcement for airplane tires. As a result, it was one of the goods subject to government **rationing.** Once rationing began, nylon stockings became scarce.

Another synthetic that found wide use in the war effort was neoprene, a synthetic rubber created in 1931. Because the Japanese had seized the rubber-growing regions of Southeast Asia, neoprene was valuable. The Allies used it to make tires for planes and land vehicles. The Germans, too, relied primarily on synthetic rubber.

Agriculture

INCREASING CROP YIELDS DURING THE DEPRESSION

The overuse of farmland coupled with severe droughts and dust storms during the early 1930s intensified Depression woes on the farm. Agricultural leaders tried to

A New Face for Mount Rushmore

In 1927 a sculptor, Gutzon Borglum, designed the 500-foot-high Mount Rushmore National Memorial in South Dakota. The sculpture shows the faces of four U.S. presidents: George Washington, Thomas Jefferson, Theodore Roosevelt, and Abraham Lincoln. Borglum supervised the work on the memorial until his death in 1941; his son completed the job.

combat these problems with better soil conservation and farming methods. During the period, more efficient machinery and improved crops were found on American farms. Chemical fertilizers, pesticides (to kill insects), and herbicides (to kill weeds) also helped revive American farming.

Under the New Deal's Agricultural Adjustment Act, the government took over the land of displaced farmers. Then it reseeded the area as grassland. Government experts urged farmers to raise such

On May 1, 1931, the Empire State Building in New York City was dedicated. At 1,250 feet high, it became the tallest building in the world and would remain so for the next 40 years. The firm Shreve, Lamb, and Harmon designed the limestone and steel building. It cost $41 million and took less than two years to build.

The new building gained added fame in 1933 when a movie depicted the giant ape King Kong scaling its heights.

Because of the country's economic crisis during the 1930s, most of the building's available space remained unrented for years. To pay the building's taxes, the owners had to rely heavily on sightseers. More than 4 million people had visited the Empire State Building by April 1940.

crops as soybeans, which manage to return **nutrients** to the soil. One method was to leave enough plant remains at harvest to hold the soil until replanting. The government also showed farmers better methods of irrigating, cultivating, and harvesting their crops.

Research helped farmers produce more from an acre than they had in the past. For example, the discovery of **hybrid** strains of corn helped increase crop yields by wide margins. Farmers all over the country were growing hybrid corn by 1943.

Other advances in research aided farmers. Cheaper fertilizers helped increase crop yields. New pesticides and herbicides helped farmers destroy bothersome insects and weeds. The new synthetic pesticide DDT was first used in 1939. DDT benefited farmers by killing a wide variety of crop-destroying insects. But DDT proved harmful to the environment and was banned in later decades. Farmers gained effective

▶ Two children demonstrate the magic of the new "miracle pen"—the ballpoint—by writing under water.

weed control in 1945 with the creation of a synthetic hormone that was a herbicide.

New machinery also helped farmers. In 1935 a completely self-propelled combine harvester was developed for harvesting grain. Operated by only one worker, the combine raised farm productivity by allowing one person to do the work of many. Special machines called "cotton strippers" replaced hand picking after 1930. In 1942 International Harvester improved the cotton stripper by introducing the spindle cotton picker. This version picked only ripe cotton; the earlier machine had picked both ripe and unripe cotton.

Technology

NEW CONSUMER GOODS

Many new consumer products were introduced during the 1930s and early 1940s, and some products were greatly improved. As a result, consumers began to see many products that are familiar today.

In 1933 the British company EMI (Electric and Musical Industries) first achieved stereophonic recording. But widespread stereo recording would not occur for two decades. Ballpoint pens, developed in 1938, came into wide use by 1943. In 1939, Clarence Birdseye marketed the first precooked frozen foods. The electric shaver and the tubeless tire were also introduced in this period.

Some of the most important developments of the period were in

radio. In 1933 Edwin Armstrong perfected FM (frequency modulation) radio. His technique conveyed sound on radio waves by changing the frequency of the carrier waves. This reduced the effects of artificial noise and natural interference and produced a high-quality sound. Radio was the subject of another advance as well: during the 1930s the communications systems used by police, airplane pilots, and military personnel were developed.

Office Machines

The electric typewriter was first mass-produced by IBM in 1935. In 1938, the first photocopier, using a process called xerography, was developed. Photocopiers were not perfected until the late 1950s, however. In 1934, photoelectric cells were used for the first time to open doors automatically. The au-tomatic doors debuted at Pennsylvania Station in New York City.

Another machine found in future offices advanced during the 1940s. John Atanasoff designed a working digital computer in 1939. IBM engineers completed another digital computer, known as the Mark I, in 1944. The first all-purpose, stored-program electronic digital computer was introduced in 1945. This early computer, called ENIAC, weighed 30 tons and stood two stories high. The computer used vacuum tubes, not microchips.

This period saw many advances in flight. At the beginning of the 1930s hydrogen-filled, gas-powered balloons were making long-distance trips. These airships were named "zeppelins" after the German engineer who developed them. Many people believed that

AMERICAN NOBEL PRIZE WINNERS, 1930–1945

Chemistry
Irving Langmuir, 1932
Harold C. Urey, 1934

Medicine or Physiology
Karl Landsteiner, 1930
Thomas H. Morgan, 1933
George R. Minot, William P. Murphy, and George H. Whipple, 1934
Otto Loewi, 1936
Albert Szent-Györgyi (Hungary–United States), 1937
Edward A. Doisy, 1943
Joseph Erlanger and Herbert S. Gasser, 1944

Physics
Carl D. Anderson, 1936
Clinton J. Davisson, 1937
Enrico Fermi, 1938
Ernest O. Lawrence, 1939
Otto Stern, 1943
Isidor Isaac Rabi, 1944
Wolfgang Pauli, 1945

Helicopter Debuts

Igor Sikorsky developed the modern helicopter. His VS-300 was built in October and November 1939 by Voight-Sikorsky Aircraft in Stratford, Connecticut. Sikorsky himself piloted the craft's first flight on July 18, 1940, at Stratford. The helicopter's flight lasted 15 minutes and 3 seconds. The VS-300 had a single main rotor and three auxiliary tail rotors for control.

streamlined. Pressurized cabins allowed them to fly higher. An automatic-pilot device was also developed in this period. These advances provided safe, long-distance commercial travel. In 1939 Pan American Airways began the first commercial flights across the Atlantic Ocean.

The Russian-born American inventor Igor Sikorsky added to the excitement in air travel. He designed the clipper flying boats, popular airplanes of the 1930s. He also built a model of a helicopter in 1939, making the first public flight in a helicopter the following year.

BREAKTHROUGHS IN THE FIGHT AGAINST DISEASE

Exciting findings in the field of medicine brought the prospect of better health. Vitamins C, B_2, and K were chemically identified, and their essential role in good nutrition was promoted. In addition, new medical technology appeared. For instance, doctors first used the cardiac catheter to examine the heart in 1941. Nevertheless, the main advances in this period were in new medicines.

The most far-reaching medical breakthrough of the period was the development of sulfa drugs. These were the first medicines that could successfully combat bacterial infections throughout the body. In 1932 a German biochemist, Gerhard Domagk, synthesized a red dye that he named "Prontosil." Later it was found to protect labo-

NEW PLANET DISCOVERED

The known solar system grew in the 1930s. It happened on February 18, 1930, when Clyde W. Tombaugh photographed Pluto.

Tombaugh was then the 24-year-old assistant to Percival Lowell at Lowell Observatory, in Flagstaff, Arizona. Using mathematical calculations, Lowell and other astronomers had predicted the existence of the planet. Tombaugh's photographic proof of Pluto's existence boosted the prestige of mathematical astronomers, especially because Pluto was so close to the estimated location.

zeppelins represented a new direction for air travel. That possibility ended, however, when the airship *Hindenburg* exploded. After crossing the Atlantic, the *Hindenburg* was approaching its landing site in Lakehurst, New Jersey, on May 6, 1937. It burst into flames, killing 36 people. This disaster occurred not long after the explosions of two other airships. The combined tragedies convinced engineers to abandon further development of airships.

Other advances in flight focused on the airplane. The progress was great: planes in the 1940s could carry more and fly farther and faster than they could in earlier decades. They could carry more because they were bigger and heavier. They could fly farther partly because they were more

ratory mice from certain bacterial infections. When Prontosil was studied further, it was found to change into the sulfa drug sulfanilamide. This substance, the first sulfa drug, was eventually used against such bacterial infections as scarlet fever and meningitis. Other sulfa drugs were rapidly introduced. They were so remarkable in combatting disease that people called them "wonder drugs."

In 1937 the French chemist Daniel Bovet discovered a group of compounds that he named "antihistamines." These drugs helped relieve sinus congestion triggered by allergies among other conditions. By 1944, the first commercial antihistamine was available to the public.

Another wonder drug was the **antibiotic** called "penicillin." Penicillin was accidentally discovered in 1928 on a mold, but it could not be isolated until the late 1930s. Penicillin was successfully used to treat a bacterial infection in 1941. Mass production of the drug began in 1943. Penicillin immediately went to the battlefield. Doctors used it to prevent infections in wounded soldiers. Its success led scientists to test other molds in the search for more antibiotics. One result was the isolation of streptomycin in 1943. In 1945 it became the first antibiotic used successfully to treat tuberculosis.

Chemists at Harvard University achieved the first total synthesis of quinine in 1944. Their quinine derivatives were used to combat malaria. In fact, the derivatives were more effective for this purpose than natural quinine itself. Their usefulness against malaria

Polio Outbreaks Terrify Americans

Epidemics of poliomyelitis (also called "polio" or "infantile paralysis") recurred annually during the 1930s. An average of 7,500 cases were recorded each year. The disease, which either killed or permanently paralyzed sufferers, had no prevention or cure during this time. It appeared in waves, usually during the late summer and autumn, and its victims were most often children.

For surviving polio victims, there was little treatment. Those who were paralyzed usually needed a wheelchair or metal leg braces to move around. People whose lungs had been paralyzed had an even grimmer fate—the iron lung. This huge and expensive device required the polio victim to lie inside it, immobile and needing constant attention.

▼ ▼ ▼

To aid polio victims, FDR helped create the Warm Springs Foundation.

President Franklin D. Roosevelt, who had been paralyzed by polio from the waist down in 1921, was an example of courage and hope for polio sufferers. His cheerful personality and the devotion of his wife, Eleanor, showed that polio need not mean the end of an active life. Photographers never took pictures of the president in his wheelchair or being lifted in and out of his specially designed car. Consequently, many Americans never realized that Roosevelt was unable to walk or stand without assistance.

was especially important during the war in the Pacific.

In 1934 the French physicists Frédéric Joliot-Curie and Irène Joliot-Curie revealed new forms of radioactive elements, now called "radioisotopes." The breakthrough created little stir in medicine at the time. In later decades, however, scientists used the isotopes to study and treat the human body. This had a tremendous impact on medicine.

DEVELOPMENTS MADE FOR WAR

Hitler's tanks rolled over Polish cavalry to open World War II. The United States dropped two devastating atomic bombs to end that war. In between, many other technological changes aided the war effort, both for attack and defense. Some of these new developments—

"Lady Lindy," the Female Flier

A newspaper headline of July 2, 1937, announced the news: EARHART DISAPPEARS! LADY LINDY LOST! So began one of the great mysteries of the century. To this day, no one knows what happened to America's most famous female flier, Amelia Earhart, and her navigator Frederick J. Noonan. Were they shot down by the Japanese? Did they crash and become cap-

tives of the Japanese while on a spy mission for the United States? Did Earhart plan her disappearance because of marital problems? Did she and Noonan survive the crash and live in obscurity somewhere? The controversy still rages. Some investigators claim to have found her plane or to have seen Japanese documents regarding her fate.

Amelia Earhart (1897–1937?) took up aviation as a hobby but soon made it her career. In 1928 she became the first woman passenger on a transatlantic flight when she flew in the plane *Friendship,* piloted by Wilmer Stultz. After a series of record-breaking transcontinental flights, Earhart became the first woman to make a solo transatlantic flight, going from Harbor Grace, Newfoundland, to Ireland in 1932. Her exploits captured the public imagi-

nation. Publisher George P. Putnam, her mentor who later became her husband, kept her name in the public eye. He arranged for her to give lectures, write books and articles, and endorse merchandise.

In June 1937 Earhart left Miami with navigator Noonan in an attempt to be the first to fly around the world near the equator. After reaching New Guinea, she took off for Howland Island in the Pacific on July 1. After that, her plane vanished. The Coast Guard cutter *Itasca* was near Howland, but lost contact with her in a confusion over radio frequencies. The lack of coordination and interference by too many people, including her husband, complicated the search that followed. A major naval search failed to find any trace of Earhart. To this day, the end of her story is unknown.

such as radar—had uses for civilian life after the war.

Much of the new war-related technology came from government research laboratories specially built to help in the war effort. Several university-based research centers also contributed to technological progress during the war. Labs at Princeton and the University of California at Berkeley are examples.

Control of the Skies

World War I had shown that control of the skies contributed to victory. Many technological changes aimed at ensuring that control. Naturally, much of that progress built on steps that had been taken before the war.

Airplane designers created huge bombers and fast fighters that had abilities unmatched before the war. Early in the war, fighters flew at 300 miles per hour and reached altitudes of about 30,000 feet. Planes flying at the end of the war could surpass those speeds and heights by 25 percent.

Perhaps the most spectacular planes were the huge, lumbering bombers. The B-17 could bomb targets 600 miles from its base. The plane held a 10-person crew, bristled with machine guns, and carried 3 tons of bombs. Covered in thick steel armor, it was nicknamed the "flying fortress." The B-17 was a huge plane—until the B-29 came along. This larger bomber, called the "superfortress," could fly two and a half times farther and carry almost twice as many bombs.

Some researchers worked on jet propulsion. In Britain, Frank Whittle had developed a jet engine as early as 1930. It was tested in 1937 and first used to power a plane in 1941. Meanwhile, in Germany, Hans von Ohain also developed a jet engine in 1935, which led to the first jet-powered flight in 1939.

The first U.S. jet airplane was tested in 1942. Called the XP-59, or Airacomet, the plane flew for the first time in an October 1, 1942, test. Pilot Robert Morris Stanley reached speeds of more than 400 miles per hour and climbed as high as 40,000 feet. Stanley found that the jet flew faster at higher altitudes. Built by the Bell Aircraft Corporation, the plane did not become a factor during the war.

Germany broke through with the Messerschmitt 262, the first jet fighter and the fastest plane known at the time. However, too few of the planes were produced, and they came too late—1944 and 1945—to influence the war's outcome. Britain's fast Gloster Meteor jets did play a significant role in the war. They successfully intercepted and shot down the V-1 "buzz bombs" that Germany launched against Britain in 1944.

Aircraft carriers became the core of the U.S. Navy's effort in the Pacific. One reason was the loss of several battleships in the attack at Pearl Harbor. Early carriers, such as the *Lexington* and *Saratoga* (built in 1927), were joined by a group of smaller and faster carriers with armor-plated hulls (*Enterprise, Yorktown,* and *Hornet*). These ships could handle larger and more powerful air squadrons.

The Japanese worried about the U.S. carriers. Because those ships were not destroyed in the

ELECTRON MICROSCOPE DEBUTS

The Radio Corporation of America (RCA) publicly tested the first electron microscope in its laboratory in Camden, New Jersey, on April 20, 1940. The amazing new instrument could magnify objects 100,000 times. This was an improvement over standard glass-lensed microscopes—they magnify only up to 2,000 times. The electron microscope uses the short wavelengths of electron beams and uses an electromagnetic field as a lens.

The first electron microscope stood about 10 feet high and weighed 700 pounds. Its earliest model was built in Berlin by Ernst Ruska and Max Knoll in 1931. That microscope could magnify an object only 17 times. The technology of the electron microscope's lens design and other features were improved greatly by the time of RCA's public test.

Today, scanning electron microscopes perform even better. These devices can produce three-dimensional images that have been magnified 1 million times.

attack at Pearl Harbor, the United States still had a powerful weapon. Indeed, the carriers were pivotal in the U.S. victories in the Coral Sea and at Midway because of their ability to launch long-range air strikes. The first bombing raid on Tokyo—in April 1942—was made by B-25s, normally land-based, taking off from the carrier *Hornet*.

Radar and Sonar

Control of the skies was not just a matter of airplanes and carriers. Radar, used to detect incoming planes, played a crucial role in defense. Sonar was used to locate submarines, making it a danger-

ous weapon. Between 1934 and 1940 Britain's Sir Robert Watson-Watt and his team developed a *ra*-*d*io *d*etecting *a*nd *r*anging (radar) system. This electronic device could detect the presence, location, bearing, and distance of enemy aircraft by bouncing radio waves off them. The British installed a radar system around the country's coast in 1935. The system proved indispensable during the Battle of Britain. Incoming German planes were detected early, and British fighters could take off to meet them. Radar sets were later fitted to naval escort vessels in convoys. They were also mounted in aircraft.

Radar has become an important part of civilian life. It is now standard equipment on commercial airliners. Air-traffic control operators also rely on radar to track planes.

Sonar was another important piece of equipment. Although first developed by British, French, and American researchers during World War I, sonar was perfected by American scientists for use in World War II. Sonar is an acronym for *s*ound *n*avigation *a*nd *r*anging. It is a system for detecting submerged submarines by means of sound waves. Radar and sonar helped the Allies gain dominance of the seas during the war.

Bombs and Rockets

Both Axis and Allied scientists developed several new bombs—and rockets. Britain's Barnes Wallis devised "shipping bombs," the most powerful bombs until the atomic bomb. They were used specifically for raids on dams and bridges. An-

▼ This sailor takes information from radar screens and marks it on a vertical chart. Radar and the airplane allowed military forces to fight over huge distances. Naval warfare was transformed into a battle of aircraft.

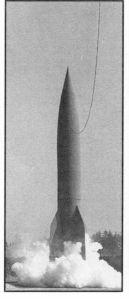

other British bomb could destroy huge slabs of concrete.

Incendiary bombs, another destructive weapon, start fires when they explode. The fires begin because the bombs contain flammable chemicals. One such chemical is napalm, which came to be used late in the war. Incendiary bombs can be devastating. The Allies' fire bombing of Dresden in 1945, for instance, destroyed much of that German city and killed tens of thousands of civilians. Critics charge that the war situation did not justify this bombing.

A major step in the use of bombs came with the invention of the proximity fuse. A fuse makes a bomb explode. The proximity fuse used radar signals to make the bomb explode a certain distance from the target. Bombs with these fuses were dropped on ground troops starting in 1944. The fuses were set to explode the bomb a certain distance above the ground, which scattered shell fragments over the soldiers. Proximity fuses improved antiaircraft weapons.

They ensured that shells exploded near enough attacking planes to cause damage. This fuse was also valuable against the German V-1 rockets.

Germany's secret weapons, the V-1 and V-2 missiles, terrorized Britain from 1944 to 1945. The V-1 was a pilotless, jet-propelled flying bomb known for its buzzing sound, hence the nickname "buzz bomb." Once the buzzing stopped, the missile nose-dived and the warhead exploded. Some 6,725 V-1s fell on Britain, killing about 6,000 people.

The V-2 missile was a liquid-filled, rocket-propelled bomb developed by Wernher von Braun. V-2s were more powerful than V-1s, could travel 3,600 miles per hour, and made no warning sound. They were also mobile; they could be launched from a platform towed by a truck and moved anywhere. Although these missiles brought further death and destruction in Britain, they did not shift the war in favor of Germany. They came too late.

▲ The three images show the launching sequence of a V-2 rocket. After the war the developer of the V-2, Wernher von Braun, moved to the United States where he later worked on the space program.

PATENTS ISSUED, 1930–1945

Fluorescent lamps, 1933
Electric blender, 1936
Cellophane tape, 1937
Ballpoint pen, 1938
DDT, 1939
Radar, 1940–1945
Oil pipelines, 1941–1945
Tubeless tire, 1942
Digital computer (ENIAC), 1944

ARTS AND ENTERTAINMENT

Both fantasy and morality play, The Wizard of Oz (above) symbolizes Hollywood's impact during these years. The Kansas scenes are shot in black and white. When Dorothy enters Oz, however, she moves into a dazzling world of color. Thus did the movie industry treat its audiences. Beaten down by joblessness and breadlines, people needed relief. Hollywood churned out splashy musicals, zany comedies, thrilling swashbucklers, and teary dramas to help America take its mind off its troubles.

Hollywood dominated arts and entertainment. Movie studios bought rights to best-selling novels. Actors, dancers, and songwriters were imported from Broadway. When the Big Band sound took off, the bands began to appear in

AT A GLANCE

- ► "Me Tarzan, You Jane"
- ► "Hooray for Hollywood"
- ► The Golden Age of Radio
- ► The World of the Theater
- ► The Big Band Era
- ► Of Mitchell and Men
- ► A New Deal for Art

movies. Even serious artists served time in Hollywood—not always happily. William Faulkner and F. Scott Fitzgerald wrote screenplays, and Aaron Copland penned movie scores.

The other major entertainment force was radio. Americans' audio door to the world, it broadcast news, sports, music, comedy, and drama. Radio brought World War II to the country's listeners. News from London during the Blitz shaped American opinion about aggressive Germany and stalwart Britain. Radio interrupted a quiet Sunday with the shocking news from Pearl Harbor. Radio and Hollywood joined in the war effort, providing both emotional release and morale-boosting tales of heroism, all wrapped in highly entertaining packages.

DATAFILE

Attendance and sales	1930	1945
Movie attendance (weekly)	90 mil.	85 mil.
Reading material sales (excluding educational)	$776 mil.	$1.5 bil.
Home audio/visual expenditures	$948 mil.	$432 mil.

The press	1930	1945
Number of daily newspapers	1,942	1,749
Circulation	39.6 mil.	48.4 mil.

	1931	1947
Number of magazines	4,887	4,610
Circulation	183.5 mil.	384.6 mil.

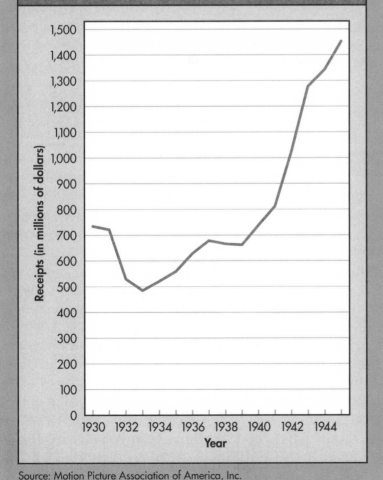

LIGHTS, CAMERA, ACTION!
Box Office Receipts for Movies, 1930–1945

Source: Motion Picture Association of America, Inc.

"ME TARZAN, YOU JANE"

Millions of Americans put aside their problems by turning to the movies, radio, funny papers, and comic books. They cheered when cartoonist Chester Gould's Dick Tracy caught the gangsters, and chuckled at the country "doin's" of Al Capp's rural folk in *Li'l Abner.* The underlying message in all these forms of entertainment was that good always triumphs over evil, and virtue brings rewards. The need to restore order in society was strong. Crime fighters succeeded in the modern city (the Green Hornet) and in the old West (the Lone Ranger).

A major trend by the mid-1930s was adventure-oriented fare that took people backward or forward in time, or to distant places. Edgar Rice Burroughs's adventures of "Tarzan, the Ape Man," were set in the faraway African jungle. By the end of the 1930s, the Tarzan character had appeared in 21 novels, a comic strip, a 15-minute daily radio serial, and 16 movies. The most well-known movie Tarzan was Olympic swimming champion Johnny Weissmuller. Cowboy star Tom Mix showed in his films and on his radio show that "lawbreakers always lose." Science fiction heroes like Flash Gordon and Buck Rogers proved that, even in outer space, good triumphs.

Equally popular were the adventures of children, often parentless, who succeeded in helping others when the authorities failed. In the funny papers and on the radio, Little Orphan Annie and her

THE MERCHANDISING OF LITTLE ORPHAN ANNIE

One of the most popular multimedia stars of the 1930s was Little Orphan Annie. Annie began as a comic strip, created by Harold Gray. Soon, Little Orphan Annie and her dog, Sandy, had their own radio serial.

Annie brought her creators financial success mostly through commercial endorsements and merchandising. The radio program was sponsored by Ovaltine, which offered secret decoder rings and memberships in Annie's fan club. Coded messages given during the broadcasts often revealed nothing more exciting than "Annie says drink your Ovaltine," but young listeners didn't seem to mind.

Merchandise, endorsements, and the original comic strip earned $100,000 in 1934 alone.

NEW SUPERHERO IS BORN

Two cartoonists, Jerry Siegel and Joe Schuster, created a new comic-book character in 1938. His name was Superman, and he was an instant success as a key character in *Action Comics*. People loved the character because he fought the powerful interests, offering hope in a time of powerlessness.

dog, Sandy, helped decent folks fight their oppressors. Five-year-old Shirley Temple became America's sweetheart after appearing in the movie *Stand Up and Cheer* in 1934. Little girls everywhere acquired two real-life heroines in 1937 when the father of Britain's young Elizabeth and Margaret became king and the two girls became royal princesses.

Mass entertainment was commercial, and many of these heroes and heroines promoted products. The Dick Tracy radio show advertised Quaker Oats. Radio's Jack Armstrong, "the All-American Boy," sold Wheaties. Sometimes manufacturers used the names of popular people or characters to market a line of products. Shirley Temple dolls, Buck Rogers disintegration guns, and Elizabeth and Margaret paper dolls were big sellers.

Movies

"HOORAY FOR HOLLYWOOD"

During the 1930s and early 1940s moviemaking became really big business. The silver screen created many magical moments, such as Fred Astaire and Ginger Rogers dancing the Continental, Greta Garbo dying as the tragic Camille, and King Kong climbing the Empire State Building. Screenwriters and producers reflected people's hopes and dreams, shaped new dreams—and sometimes gave their audiences social and political themes to ponder.

At the end of the 1930s, each major studio—MGM, Paramount, 20th Century-Fox, Warner Brothers, RKO, Columbia, and Universal—turned out more than 50 films a year. Smaller studios specialized. Walt Disney produced animated films, and Republic produced low-budget westerns. To shoot these movies, studios built huge soundstages and several standing sets that covered hundreds of acres. People bought about 80 million movie tickets a week.

Films and Stars

Talking movies replaced silent films in the late 1920s, and the "talkie" craze helped protect Hollywood from economic setback in the early 1930s. Universal scored with two classic horror films in 1931, *Frankenstein*, with Boris Karloff, and *Dracula*, with Bela Lugosi. Early gangster movies were hot with Edward G. Robinson in *Little Caesar* (1930), James Cagney in *Public Enemy* (1931), and Paul Muni as Al Capone in *Scarface* (1932). Also heating up the screen were the blonde "sex goddesses" Jean Harlow, Marlene Dietrich, and Mae West. Harlow was a product of MGM's star-making system. The studio first cast her in bad-girl roles in films such as *Hell's Angels*, and then refined her image in such films as *Saratoga* (1937). Dietrich, known for her gorgeous legs and husky voice, skyrocketed to fame in the German movie *The Blue Angel* (1930). Mae West broke box office records with her 1933 films *She Done Him Wrong* and *I'm No Angel*. West's screen image rested on her earthy manner, sultry voice, and rule-breaking behavior.

The age of the family movie dawned in 1934, when Roman Catholic bishops formed the Legion of Decency to keep movie scenes and scripts clean. Hollywood studios cooperated by enforcing their own production code (called the "Hays Code"), which had been established in 1922 as a self-regulating guide for the industry. The code contained a long list of taboos, including long kisses, words like *hell*, and naked babies. After 1934 all films that passed code censorship received a seal of approval.

Film directors working in the 1930s built their family movies

The Studio System: Assembly-Line Art

▲ Ginger Rogers and Fred Astaire made a series of successful movies for RKO; later Astaire moved to MGM. His success disproved an early assessment of his talent: "Can't act. Can't sing. Slightly bald. Can dance a little."

From the 1920s to the early 1950s, the motion picture industry operated under the "studio system," a fast and efficient method for mass-producing movies. At each studio, a production head, such as the brilliant Irving Thalberg at Metro-Goldwyn-Mayer (MGM), supervised all movies. These authoritarian chiefs made all artistic as well as all practical decisions. Formula films that followed set patterns and film series, such as the "Tarzan" and "Dr. Kildare" movies, became standard fare. Because studios assigned directors to films, each director learned to work in a variety of genres. Some—like Frank Capra and John Ford—put their own individual stamp on films while managing to work within the system.

Each studio kept its own "stable" of directors, writers, designers, and other specialists. Each studio created its own look and style, often focusing on certain types of films. MGM was known for its glamorous look and family entertainment; Warner Brothers for its realism, gangster movies, and musicals; and Universal for its horror films.

The stars belonged to the studios, too, and their careers were shaped by the studios' desires. Roles were handed out—and careers determined—by the studio managers. The studios manipulated the stars' image by employing busy publicity departments that passed out flattering stories—and covered up any hint of scandal. MGM had most of the biggest stars, including such box-office favorites as Clark Gable and Joan Crawford. Louis B. Mayer, head of MGM, saw the studio as a family: he was the father, and the stars were his children. The stars often chafed at this paternalistic attitude.

By the 1930s the studios had gained control of all aspects of the film industry by handling distribution as well as production and by acquiring many theaters themselves. Moviemaking had become highly profitable and was increasingly under the control of big business and bankers rather than the artistic community. This monopoly led to legal troubles with the federal government by the late 1940s.

▼ Shirley Temple—shown here dancing with the great tap dancer Bill Robinson—suffered the fate of many child stars. Although she was the top box office draw for years, her acting career ended when she grew up.

around comedy, music, and some forceful drama. They served up a number of smash hits featuring child performers, whose innocence and ability to help others appealed to Depression-weary people. Young Shirley Temple reigned as top box office star from 1935 to 1938. At the end of the decade Mickey Rooney zoomed to the top with the "Andy Hardy" film series, in which he played a romanticized version of the typical American teenager. Other child stars like Jackie Cooper, Margaret O'Brien, and Britishers Roddy McDowall and Elizabeth Taylor also became public favorites.

Comic stars included the Marx Brothers, Laurel and Hardy, and W. C. Fields. A new genre that combined comedy and romance—called "screwball" comedy—arose. Cary Grant was the master. The favorite comedy of the decade was Frank Capra's *It Happened One Night* (1934), starring Clark Gable as an out-of-work newspaperman traveling with runaway heiress Claudette Colbert across country by bus.

Musicals thrived in the thirties. Director Busby Berkeley staged huge spectacles for such movies as *Gold Diggers of 1933*, and Jeanette MacDonald and Nelson Eddy sang film operettas. The champions of the musical were Fred Astaire and Ginger Rogers, the song-and-dance team who brought romance and elegance to the screen with such hits as *Top Hat* and *Swing Time*.

Female stars included the versatile Bette Davis, who portrayed a prostitute in *Of Human Bondage,* a femme fatale in *Jezebel,* and a queen in *The Private Lives of Elizabeth and Essex.* Katharine Hepburn was another leading lady of film, taking both dramatic and comic roles. Among the male stars, Gary Cooper was the strong, silent type; Humphrey Bogart the principled tough guy; Errol Flynn the swashbuckler; and Spencer Tracy the chameleon, who could play any role. But the "king" of Hollywood was Clark Gable. His presence helped make *Gone with the Wind* (1939) one of the most popular movies of all time.

Three of the great moviemakers of the era were Walt Disney, Frank Capra, and Orson Welles. Disney produced the first full-length animated film, *Snow White and the Seven Dwarfs.* His innovative *Fantasia* (1940) linked animation with classical music. Of course, Disney's studio also created countless short features starring the popular Mickey Mouse. The first director to win three Oscars, Capra used his films to celebrate democracy and the common man. His typical hero is an honest, naive American who triumphs over evil because of his wit, courage, and goodness. Gary Cooper helped the Depression jobless in *Mr. Deeds Goes to Town*, and stopped a power-hungry industrialist in *Meet John Doe*. Jimmy Stewart attacked corrupt politicians in *Mr. Smith Goes to Washington*. Welles was a brilliant experimenter. His *Citizen Kane* (1941)—which he cowrote, directed, and starred in—is a masterpiece of light and shadow.

Hollywood Goes to War

As war clouds gathered over Europe, the movie industry drew plots from the international scene. Early war-based movies helped prepare Americans for conflict. In 1940 Alfred Hitchcock's *Foreign Correspondent* warned, "Don't let the lights go out all over Europe." *Mrs. Miniver* (1942) portrayed the gallant British; *Casablanca* (1942) showed how freedom-loving people could resist Nazi aggression.

When war came, Hollywood pitched in. Many stars, including Clark Gable, Jimmy Stewart, and Robert Taylor, joined the armed services. Directors traveled to battlefields to film documentaries on the war. On the home front many stars joined together to start the Hollywood Canteen, where soldiers and sailors could dance with their favorite stars. The United Services Organization (USO) grew out of the canteen and began sending entertainers like Bob Hope to perform for troops stationed overseas.

Hollywood did produce a number of war films. Some were realistic—like *Bataan*—but most were sentimental stories meant to stir patriotic feelings. Mostly the public

▲ The USO sent entertainers everywhere during the war— even to this makeshift stage on an aircraft carrier's flight deck.

wanted to be entertained. Such comedies as *The Philadelphia Story*, with Katharine Hepburn, Cary Grant, and Jimmy Stewart, and *Going My Way*, with Bing Crosby, scored hits. Big musicals starred Judy Garland in the nostalgic *Meet Me in St. Louis* and Crosby and Fred Astaire in the sentimental *Holiday Inn*. That film introduced "White Christmas," a song that became a holiday standard. Sometimes entertainment and the war effort were combined. James Cagney's *Yankee Doodle Dandy* and Laurence Olivier's *Henry V* used music and Shakespeare to rouse patriotism.

GOLDWYNISMS

A top producer of family films was MGM's Samuel Goldwyn Jr., known for his fractured language. Legend has him commenting on the pitfalls of deal making: "A verbal contract isn't worth the paper it's written on."

Radio

THE GOLDEN AGE OF RADIO

Radio provided Americans with the cheapest and most varied entertainment available during the Depression and World War II. People could enjoy dramas, musical programs, comedies, and adventure series as well as keep up with the news in the comfort of their homes. Listeners were also bombarded with sales pitches for all sorts of products; radio became thoroughly commercialized during this period.

Hit Shows

People tuned in every Thursday night to hear Kate Smith, "Songbird of the South," and every Saturday to *Your Hit Parade* to hear the top ten songs of the week. They listened to Bing Crosby croon, Ar-

▼ Essential for the success of many radio shows, the sound effects crew awaits its cues from the two actresses in the foreground.

turo Toscanini conduct the NBC Symphony, and their favorite Big Bands play swing.

Every day millions of people would gather to hear the latest chapter in their favorite serial dramas, such as *Our Gal Sunday, Helen Trent,* and *One Man's Family.* By the end of the 1930s there were some 40 of these soap operas, so called because their sponsors were soap companies. Each unfolded the tragedies, triumphs, and scandals of life.

Laughter came from the comedy shows of Jack Benny, George Burns and Gracie Allen, and ventriloquist Edgar Bergen and his dummy Charlie McCarthy. Charlie McCarthy was so real to people—and so popular—that Prime Minister Churchill shook the dummy's hand when he met Bergen. The most popular radio show of the decade was *Amos 'n' Andy,* with white actors Freeman Gosden (Amos) and Charles Correll (Andy) playing blacks. Every weekday evening from 7:00 to 7:15 restaurants stopped serving, theaters turned off projectors, and 30 million Americans tuned in to hear the latest episode. White Americans loved the show because the characters were unthreatening bunglers with never-ending get-rich-quick schemes. Many blacks hated it, with good cause. It continued white stereotypes about blacks and made black people targets for laughter.

Radio emerged as an important source of news and information. One of the most successful news shows was the weekly *March of Time.* During World War II, reporters brought the war into every home. Eight days after Pearl Harbor, Norman Cousins's "We Hold These Truths" was heard by 40 million people, the largest audience ever to hear a dramatic program on radio.

Invasion from Mars

As panicked Americans clogged highways to escape the "invasion," the radio announcer continued: "I'm speaking from the roof of the Broadcasting Building in New York City. The bells you hear are ringing to warn people to evacuate the city as the Martians approach. . . . Our army [is] wiped out . . . artillery, air force, everything [is] wiped out. This may be the last broadcast." This dire report was part of the most incredible radio show of the century, broadcast the night before Halloween in 1938.

The radio play *Invasion from Mars*, written by Howard Koch and starring Orson Welles, contained a series of news broadcasts announcing that invading Martians had landed in New Jersey and were destroying everything in sight with death rays. Unfortunately, the broadcast was so realistic that people believed it. It took days for the panic to subside.

Propaganda on the Air

Just as Roosevelt had discovered the importance of radio as a political tool, so various other public figures used the airwaves to push their own ideas. Louisiana governor Huey Long used radio to organize his "Share Our Wealth" movement. Father Charles E. Coughlin was successful in promoting his political views on the radio until the mid-1940s, when protests

Reporting the War

◄ Edward R. Murrow prepares a news report at CBS News headquarters in London.

Correspondents reporting via radio and newspapers brought the facts, sounds, sights, images, and feel of World War II into American homes every day. Many of these reporters, including Edward R. Murrow, H. V. Kaltenborn, and Ernie Pyle, became famous personalities. Each in his own way had a special ability to present the news, boost morale, and give a personal perspective on the unfolding events.

Murrow headed the European news effort for the Columbia Broadcasting System (CBS). In 1938 he and William L. Shirer delivered 18 days (from September 12 to 29) of blow-by-blow accounts of the diplomatic maneuverings at the Munich Conference. In that same span of time,

Kaltenborn made more than 80 broadcasts to tie together their reports and give his own personal view of the events and men involved. Hitler, Kaltenborn said, was a difficult "man of moods." Later, the tension in Murrow's voice and the detail he provided in his live broadcasts during the German air raids conveyed the terror and destruction of the London Blitz.

The wartime reports of Ernie Pyle, champion of the GI, were syndicated in some 300 newspapers nationwide. A Pulitzer Prize winner, Pyle reported from the front lines of the land wars in North Africa, Italy, and France and ground fighting in the Pacific. His stories gave Americans a true-to-life portrait of the infantry, whom he described as "the mud-rain-frost-and-wind boys . . . the guys that wars can't be won without." American soldiers and civilians alike mourned when Pyle was killed in 1945 by a sniper near Okinawa.

The comedy duo of George Burns and Gracie Allen easily shifted from vaudeville to radio in the early thirties. Their first regular program began in 1932 on CBS, and they remained one of the top-rated radio programs during the 1930s.

George and Gracie's comedy was based on their characters: Gracie was the eternal scatterbrain with a muddled vocabulary, and George was her flustered boyfriend and straight man. (They were married in real life.) In a typical exchange from their show, George asked Gracie if something had happened to her when she was a baby. Gracie replied: "When I was born, I was so surprised I couldn't talk for a year and a half."

BIRTHS . . .

Stephen Sondheim, composer, 1930
Elvis Presley, singer, 1935
Woody Allen, filmmaker, 1935
Joan Baez, singer, 1941
John Irving, novelist, 1942
Alice Walker, novelist, 1941

. . . AND DEATHS

Lon Chaney, actor, 1930
John Philip Sousa, "March King," 1932
Florenz Ziegfeld, producer, 1932
George Gershwin, composer, 1937
Jean Harlow, actress, 1937
F. Scott Fitzgerald, novelist, 1940

against his radical ideas forced him off the air. During the 1930s Coughlin broadcast every Sunday from the Shrine of the Little Flower in Royal Oak, Michigan, delivering angry attacks against communists, "Jewish bankers," and labor unions. He thought that the New Deal leaned toward communism, and he labeled FDR "Franklin Double-Crossing Roosevelt" and the "great betrayer and liar." At his peak, Coughlin was second only to Roosevelt as an effective speaker.

Theater

THE WORLD OF THE THEATER

In the 1930s theater audiences dwindled and productions became increasingly difficult to finance. However, the theater got new life from social protest dramas and the emergence of new theatrical groups that offered low-priced productions of challenging plays by new writers. Plays exploring social and political issues appeared along with lighter Broadway fare.

Eugene O'Neill continued as the master American playwright with his long tragedy *Mourning Becomes Electra* (1931) and the nostalgic comedy *Ah, Wilderness!* (1933). In 1938 Thornton Wilder presented *Our Town*, one of the most original plays of the modern stage. A re-creation of small-town American life, the drama focuses on the universal problems of living and dying and uses the dramatic technique of a stage manager to control the action.

Theater of Social Protest

Much of the serious, challenging drama of the era was performed in workers' theaters, playhouses of the Federal Theatre Project, and other new kinds of theater groups. The Labor Stage was founded by New York members of the International Ladies Garment Workers Union. Among other works, it presented the successful musical revue *Pins and Needles* (1937–1940), which satirized everything—Nazis, fascists, communists, bigots, and even unions. New York City's Group Theatre, founded in 1931, became America's premiere ensemble acting company and presented plays of social criticism. Acclaimed new playwright Clifford Odets wrote powerful, realistic dramas for the Group Theatre. His *Golden Boy* (1937) attacked materialism through the success story of a musician-turned-boxer.

Other major dramatists of the period also dealt with social issues. Noted for his verse dramas, Maxwell Anderson exposed social injustice in his powerful tragedy *Winterset* (1935) and depicted fascism as the challenge of the age in *Key Largo* (1938). At the peak of his creative talent, Robert Sherwood triumphed with his play on gangster terror, *The Petrified Forest* (1934), and his tragicomedy on the insanity of war, *Idiot's Delight* (1935).

America's foremost female playwright, Lillian Hellman, burst onto the stage with a controversial psychological drama, *The Children's Hour*, in 1934. Her most famous play, *The Little Foxes* (1938), was a study of greed and family life in the industrialized South.

On Broadway

Broadway hardly reflected the Depression from 1930 to 1933 when it offered such lavish shows as Florenz Ziegfeld's *Follies*, Earl Carroll's *Vanities*, and George White's *Scandals.* George and Ira Gershwin's light but biting satire of a presidential election, *Of Thee I Sing*, won a Pulitzer Prize, and George S. Kaufman's *Dinner at Eight* was a comedy hit. Other successful comedies in the 1930s were Philip Barry's *The Philadelphia Story* (1938) and two plays by Kaufman and Moss Hart: *I'd Rather Be Right*, a satire of FDR's troubles with the Supreme Court, and *The Man Who Came to Dinner* (1939).

Musicals were extremely popular throughout the decade. In 1932 Irving Berlin's *Face the Music* and Cole Porter's *Gay Divorce* triumphed. Porter continued writing such hits as *Anything Goes* (1935) and *Red Hot and Blue* (1936), both starring the queen of musical comedy, Ethel Merman. The partnership of composer Richard Rodgers and lyricist Lorenz Hart created such popular shows as *On Your Toes* (1936) and *The Boys from Syracuse* (1938). One of the most original musicals was Gershwin's *Porgy and Bess* (1935), an American black folk opera that combined elements of jazz and opera.

Theater During World War II

By 1941 the movement that produced the Group Theatre and labor theaters was dead, and social dramas were out of favor. Comedies, such as William Saroyan's *The Time of Your Life* and Harold Lindsey and Russell Crouse's *Life*

Federal Theatre Project

Between 1935 and 1939, the Federal Theatre, established under the New Deal's WPA, employed about 10,000 performers, directors, writers, and designers. Together these theater professionals brought the stage to more than 30 million people in 29 states. Under the national direction of Hallie Flanagan, drama professor and director of the Vassar Experimental Theatre, the project stimulated a new growth and appreciation for theater. It also became a thorny political issue. Many conservatives objected to the tolerant attitudes the project's stage productions often took toward labor, minorities, and aliens. By 1939 the project was viewed as too extreme; Congress abolished it in June of that year.

During its lifetime, the Federal Theatre presented a wide range of stage fare. It revived many of the classics and created some 77 new plays. The new productions included religious, foreign-language, ethnic, and children's productions, along with puppet shows, vaudeville, and dance programs. Two works—*Voodoo Macbeth* staged by an all-black cast, directed by Orson Welles, and the antifascist play *It Can't Happen Here* by Sinclair Lewis—received special acclaim. An important aspect of the project was the flourishing of black theater in many cities. One successful production was *The Swing Mikado*, a black jazz version of Gilbert and Sullivan's operetta.

▼ ▼ ▼

The Federal Theatre Project was part of the Works Progress Administration.

The Living Newspaper, a collectively written, documentary-style play focusing on social and economic issues, grew up inside the Federal Theatre Project. These thought-provoking and imaginative "plays" featured visual aids, folk humor, and training films and furthered the development of educational radio. Two of the most successful *Living Newspapers* were *Power*, about the Tennessee Valley Authority, and *One-Third of a Nation*, about Depression economics.

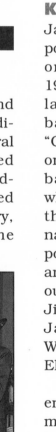

▼ This gathering of swing greats includes (from left) singer Dinah Shore, comic musician Spike Jones, trumpeter Bob Burns, pianist Count Basie, vibraphone player Lionel Hampton, and trombonist Tommy Dorsey.

with Father, were hits. In 1945 one of America's greatest playwrights, Tennessee Williams, moved onto center stage and changed the pace of stage fare with his haunting drama *The Glass Menagerie.* But the big stage news was what happened to the musical. Richard Rodgers and Oscar Hammerstein transformed musical comedy by making dance sequences part of the plot for the first time in their hit shows *Oklahoma!* (1943) and *Carousel* (1945).

Music

THE BIG BAND ERA

During the 1930s both radio and records greatly widened the audience for music. The WPA's Federal Music Project alone sponsored 14,000 radio broadcasts. By mid-decade a new style of jazz called "swing" was sweeping the country, thanks to the Big Bands of the era. Swing was a dance-oriented version of jazz, based on the individual techniques of musicians and a "swinging" rhythmic pattern. Earlier jazz had been performed primarily by small groups of black musicians, but the Swing Era (1937–1947) brought jazz into the mainstream of American music. Each Big Band typically featured a rhythm section of piano, double bass, drums, and guitar with five saxophones, three or four trumpets, three or four trombones, and perhaps a clarinet or flute. Most bands also had vocalists.

Kings of Swing

Jazz clarinetist Benny Goodman, popularly crowned "King of Swing," organized his famous band in 1934. Goodman made swing popular across the nation when his band played such hit songs as "Goody Goody" and "Blue Moon" on radio. One of the most popular bands was led by Glenn Miller, whose list of hit songs included "In the Mood" and "Moonlight Serenade." Bandleader Tommy Dorsey popularized such tunes as "Marie" and "I'll Never Smile Again." Other outstanding big bands were led by Jimmy Dorsey, Artie Shaw, Harry James, and black musicians William "Count" Basie and Duke Ellington.

By the end of the decade several white bandleaders like Goodman and Shaw had fully integrated bands with black musicians. These bands often encountered racism on the road. Swing gained more respectability when Goodman, Shaw, and other bandleaders were invited to give concerts at New York City's famed Carnegie Hall.

Swing music produced a new dance, the jitterbug, and a special language derived from African-American slang, jive talk. The jitterbug was an athletic, often acrobatic dance with "breakaways," where partners separated and improvised steps. The "shiners" (jitterbug dancers) were "in the groove" (carried away by swing) while "cuttin' the rug" (dancing) as the "cats" (musicians) and "canaries" (vocalists) performed. Two of the popular "canaries" were Helen O'Connell, who was white, and Billie Holiday, who was black. Many listeners considered Holiday the greatest jazz singer of all time; she sang with Goodman, Shaw, and Basie, and had a brilliant career on her own.

By the early 1940s, black musicians introduced a new jazz form with more complex rhythms than swing, called "Bebop" (Bop). Popularized by such performers as trumpeter Dizzy Gillespie, Bebop revitalized jazz, which developed separately from swing.

Duke Ellington: Sophisticated Master of Jazz

◄ Jazz composer and bandleader Duke Ellington leads his band from the piano in 1945.

Edward Kennedy Ellington (1899–1974) was a giant in the world of jazz. His career as pianist, composer, and bandleader spanned over 50 years. He acquired the nickname "Duke" during his teens because of his sophisticated dress, manner, and speech. In 1923 Ellington formed the first band to play complex jazz that was scored as well as improvised. Prior to Ellington's revolutionary concept, jazz was played by just four or five musicians who only improvised.

The Duke Ellington Band played at the Kentucky Club (from 1923 to 1927) and the Cotton Club (1927 to 1931) in New York City. National fame followed Ellington's radio broadcasts from the Cotton Club. A 1933 European tour gave the band an international following, and starting in 1943 the band began making annual appearances at New York's Carnegie Hall. The band was known for its instrumental soloists and for Ellington's hot, sensual, sophisticated style, which he called "jungle music."

As a composer, Ellington wrote and arranged music that was suited to the individual styles of his musicians. Some of his hit songs were "Mood Indigo," "Sophisticated Lady," "Satin Doll," and "Take the 'A' Train." He also wrote suites like "Black, Brown and Beige" (1943, a panorama of black history in the United States); a ballet score, "The River" (1970); and a Broadway musical, "Beggar's Holiday" (1947). Since Duke's death, his son, Mercer Ellington, has led the band.

▲ Simply called "The Voice," Frank Sinatra rose to stardom in the 1940s.

MARIAN ANDERSON AT LINCOLN MEMORIAL

The contralto Marian Anderson became the center of a controversy in 1939. The Daughters of the American Revolution (DAR) owned Constitution Hall in Washington, D.C. Anderson asked to perform there, but the DAR refused because she was black.

Outraged at the news, Eleanor Roosevelt resigned from the DAR and helped arrange for Anderson to give a concert at the Lincoln Memorial, which was a huge success.

Tin Pan Alley

The period was marked by an outpouring of great songs penned by such talented songwriters as the brothers George and Ira Gershwin and Cole Porter. Leading them all was Irving Berlin, whose hits included both "White Christmas" and "God Bless America."

The singing phenomenon of the 1940s was a skinny young man with intense blue eyes from Hoboken, New Jersey. His name was Frank Sinatra. Discovered in 1939 by bandleader Harry James, Sinatra gained national attention while recording a series of hit songs with the Tommy Dorsey band. When he gave his first solo concert at the Paramount Theatre in New York City in 1942, teenage girls went wild. Fans hounded

him for autographs, some trying to tear off his clothes. In 1944 riot police tried to control over 10,000 screaming "bobby-soxers" in line for concert tickets. No other entertainer had ever inspired such wild devotion.

Classical Music

Winner of the 1945 Pulitzer Prize, Aaron Copland composed classical works that incorporated jazz and folk tunes for a distinctly American sound. He wrote symphonies and piano works but may be best known for his ballet suites "Billy the Kid" (1938; choreography, Eugene Loring) and "Appalachian Spring" (1944; choreography, Martha Graham). Another major composer of the period was Samuel Barber, whose "Adagio for Strings" (1938) has become a classic of modern music.

Arturo Toscanini, called "The Maestro," was one of the greatest conductors of the century. He conducted the New York Philharmonic periodically from 1926 to 1936. In 1937 NBC created its symphony orchestra for him. He made that orchestra the most famous in the country. Another noted conductor—Leopold Stokowski—brought classical music to popular art forms. He led the orchestra that provided the music for Disney's *Fantasia.*

The black opera singer Marian Anderson, noted for her singing of spirituals, overcame discrimination and rose to international stardom during the 1930s. After hearing her sing in 1935, Toscanini said, "What I have heard today, one is privileged to listen to once in a hundred years."

Books

OF MITCHELL AND MEN

Fiction and poetry of the 1930s and the war years continued the 1920s' trend toward realism, naturalism, psychology, and experimentation. Serious writers saw the human race as the product of biologic and economic forces that continually pull it in all directions as it strives to endure in a world of constant change. Romance and adventure dominated the best-seller lists in popular fiction.

Trends in Fiction and Nonfiction

The most successful novel of the time was Margaret Mitchell's Civil War romance *Gone with the Wind* (1936), which won the Pulitzer Prize in 1937. Mitchell wrote the book while recovering from an ankle injury. Despite her claim that the novel was "pretty terrible," it earned over $1 million in royalties and movie rights in just two years.

Nonfiction sold well, too. Dale Carnegie's *How to Win Friends and Influence People* (1936) was an overnight success. It has become the second-best-selling nonfiction work of modern times, trailing only the Bible. Another critically acclaimed nonfiction work was Carl Sandburg's Pulitzer Prize–winning biography *Abraham Lincoln: The War Years.*

Three of America's most acclaimed writers produced major works during this period. F. Scott Fitzgerald's realistic portrait of mental anguish among Americans living in Paris, *Tender Is the Night*, was published in 1934. William Faulkner continued his exploration of the Southern psyche with *Light in August* (1932), which was noted for its superb characterization and symbolic prose style. Ernest Hemingway's *For Whom the Bell Tolls* (1940), based on the author's experiences during the Spanish Civil War, introduced readers to Robert Jordan, another defiant, courageous Hemingway hero.

Other important novels focused on social themes. Aldous Huxley's social satire *Brave New World* (1932) described a futuristic society where science is king. Humans are mass-produced in test tubes,

Gone with the Wind: Successful Book and Movie

Gone with the Wind, published in 1936, was one of the biggest literary successes of all time. The potboiler romance was set in the South during the Civil War and Reconstruction. Not only did it earn Margaret Mitchell huge sums in royalties and movie rights but it also won the Pulitzer Prize for fiction and was translated into 30 languages.

The long-awaited film version of *Gone with the Wind,* released in 1939, was equally successful. Fan magazines debated for months who would play Rhett and Scarlett. The final choices—Clark Gable and Vivien Leigh (above)—seem to have satisfied moviegoers for years. Some thought making the movie was a gamble, costing $4 million to produce and taking over three and a half hours to show. But the result was a triumph both financially and artistically. The film won ten Oscars. Hattie McDaniel, winner of the award for Best Supporting Actress, was the first black to win an Oscar.

conditioned to be intellectuals or workers, and kept drugged to maintain stability. Black writer Richard Wright gave a powerful portrait of the black man in white society in his 1940 novel *Native Son*. Pearl S. Buck realistically described the life of a Chinese peasant family in *The Good Earth*. This novel helped win Buck the Nobel Prize for literature in 1938.

Popular fiction saw the birth of a new genre—the hard-boiled detective novel, which emerged from the typewriters of Dashiell Hammett and Raymond Chandler. Hammett's *The Maltese Falcon* and *The Thin Man*—naturally—were turned into movies. The film versions became classics.

The hot property of the era, though, was John Steinbeck. He dominated the literary scene with several powerful novels of social protest: *Tortilla Flat* (1935), *Of Mice and Men* (1937), and *Cannery Row* (1945). His greatest work was *The Grapes of Wrath* (1939; Pulitzer Prize, 1940), which followed the plight of the Joad family as they migrated from the Dust Bowl to California and finally endured death, disease, and starvation. Like other successful books, including many of Steinbeck's, it was turned into a movie.

Poetry

Carl Sandburg and W. H. Auden set the pace for poetry throughout the 1930s. In his collection, *The People, Yes* (1936), Sandburg celebrated America by affirming his faith in democracy and in the human ability to endure. His bold, conversational style captured the pulse of American life. Anglo-American Auden was considered the principal poet of his generation. His poetry is known for its wit, quality of unexpectedness, intelligence, and focus on love as the force that gives life meaning. In one of his most famous poems, "September 1, 1939," he ponders the moral state of the world and concludes that "we must love one another or die."

The early 1940s saw the emergence of the poets Karl Shapiro, Theodore Roethke, and Randall Jarrell. Much of the early poetry of Shapiro and Jarrell deals with the war. Shapiro's great war poem "Elegy for a Dead Soldier" universalizes death. Jarrell's famous five-line poem, "The Death of the Ball Turret Gunner," stuns with horrible images.

Selected Popular Fiction, 1930–1945

Year	Title	Author
1930	Cimarron	Edna Ferber
1931	The Good Earth	Pearl S. Buck
1932	Sons	Pearl S. Buck
1933	Anthony Adverse	Hervey Allen
1934	Lamb in His Bosom	Caroline Miller
1935	Green Light	Lloyd C. Douglas
1936	Gone with the Wind	Margaret Mitchell
1937	Northwest Passage	Kenneth Roberts
1938	The Yearling	Marjorie Kinnan Rawlings
1939	The Grapes of Wrath	John Steinbeck
1940	How Green Was My Valley	Richard Llewellyn
1941	The Keys of the Kingdom	A. J. Cronin
1942	The Song of Bernadette	Franz Werfel
1943	The Robe	Lloyd C. Douglas
1944	Strange Fruit	Lillian Smith
1945	Forever Amber	Kathleen Winsor

Art

A NEW DEAL FOR ART

During the 1930s American art went through a major transformation. One reason for the changes was that the federal government, through the Federal Art Project of the WPA, began to fund art. The project made art part of America and developed the talents of many artists, like Jackson Pollock. By 1939 project artists had completed 1,300 murals, 48,100 paintings, 3,562 sculptures, and many more works. These efforts graced public buildings being constructed by the WPA.

Artists of the 1930s embraced realism and set out to rediscover America—its history, people, and culture. Regionalists like Thomas Hart Benton, John Steuart Curry, and Grant Wood championed rural America in the West, South, and Midwest. Social realists such as Charles Burchfield, Reginald Marsh, and Edward Hopper focused on the bleak, harsh side of urban life. Burchfield often concentrated on buildings and streets rather than on people. *His Ice Glare* shows broken-down buildings at a city street crossing in winter. Marsh's vivid paintings of New York City, like his dingy subway in *Why Not Use the 'L'?*, often stressed the dark side of city life. The starkness of Hopper's paintings, as in the deserted street of *Early Sunday Morning*, reveals his view of the city as a lonely place.

The movement called Art Deco reached its peak during the decade. Its streamlined, geometric designs and often exotic, decorative style

influenced crafts, interior design, and fashions. Even architecture was affected, as in the Chrysler Building in New York City. The style could also be easily adapted to new materials like plastics.

The dominant style in architecture was "streamlined moderne," which stressed simplicity, lots of glass windows, smooth surfaces, and little decoration. Classical and gothic revival architecture, which also continued to be popular, reflected a new emphasis on simplicity and less detail—as in the Jefferson Memorial in Washington, D.C.

In the 1940s New York City became the center of exciting new activity in art. This was partly due to new ideas introduced by European artists fleeing Nazi persecution. A group of artists, including Jackson Pollock, Willem de Kooning, Ad Reinhardt, and Mark Rothko, emerged early in the decade. Loosely referred to as the New York School, they became the leaders of the abstract expressionist movement of the late 1940s.

▲ Dorothea Lange, who took this picture of Texas migrants, helped document the suffering of the Depression with realistic photographs that are regarded as art.

WRIGHT DESIGNS FALLINGWATER

In 1937 the architect Frank Lloyd Wright produced one of his most famous home designs—Fallingwater, built near Bear Run, Pennsylvania.

The house drew much attention because it was built directly over a waterfall and complemented the rugged mountainside. Fallingwater is a good example of Wright's belief that buildings can link people with each other and with the natural environment. Although designed as a private home, Fallingwater is currently open to the public.

SPORTS AND LEISURE

With his smooth grace, professional manner, and unrivaled skill, Joe DiMaggio thrilled baseball fans and became a hero to all Americans. Playing in a troubled era, "Joltin' Joe" helped cheer Americans plagued by the heartache of the Depression. When war broke out, he—like thousands of other Americans, including many athletes—joined the armed forces.

Sports offered other heroes in these troubled times. Other baseball stars included Lou Gehrig and Bob Feller. Boxing was dominated by the "Brown Bomber," Joe Louis. Americans thrilled to the Olympic gold medal performances of Sonja Henie in ice skating and both Babe Didrikson (Zaharias) and Jesse Owens in track and field.

AT A GLANCE

- ▶ All-Stars and Hall of Famers
- ▶ Bowl Games and the NFL
- ▶ Owens Versus Hitler
- ▶ Louis Rules the Roost
- ▶ New Stars Net Popularity
- ▶ The Spread of Tournaments
- ▶ The Effect of the War
- ▶ America at Rest

Radio helped create these heroes. By broadcasting sporting events nationwide, radio brought the great performances of star athletes into the home with the excitement of live broadcasts. Radio news programs told people who were not even sports fans about these athletes.

Magazines helped people escape from their cares with illustrated glimpses into the lives and exploits of well-known entertainers, sports personalities, and wealthy society "stars." Millions of people explored the worlds of science and technology exhibited at two World's Fairs, one in Chicago and one in New York. Both fairs celebrated an optimistic future. The 1940s also confirmed the rise of the teenager as a specific target in the leisure-time market.

DATAFILE

Sports

World records as of 1945	Men	Women
Track and field		
100-yd. dash	9.4″	10.4″
Mile	4′01.3″	5′15.3″
High jump	6.9 ft.	5.6 ft.
Swimming		
100-m. freestyle	57.2″	1′06.8″

Leisure

	1930	1945
Average workweek	42.1 hrs.	43.5 hrs.
Attendance		
Baseball (major leagues)	10.3 mil.	11.2 mil.
Football (NFL)	492,684 (1934)	1.3 mil.
National parks	2.8 mil.	4.5 mil.
Bicycle sales	310,000	1.3 mil.

PLAY BALL!
Money Spent on Spectator Sports, 1930–1945

ALL-STARS AND HALL OF FAMERS

Both major- and minor-league baseball suffered economic setbacks during the Depression. At least five major-league teams lost money every year from 1931 to 1939. However, the reputation of the game remained clean under the forceful rule of baseball's first commissioner, Judge Kenesaw Mountain Landis (1920–1944).

The Depression saw the beginning of many baseball traditions. The first All-Star Game between the outstanding players of the American League and the National League was played in Comiskey Park, Chicago, in 1933. The first night games were introduced during the 1935 season; they gave a big boost to the game's attendance. In 1939 the National Baseball Hall of Fame was founded in Cooperstown, New York, the town where legend says that Abner Doubleday first invented the game 100 years earlier.

Because major-league baseball continued its white-only policy, blacks continued to play in the Negro leagues. Those leagues reorganized in the mid-1930s to form the Negro American and Negro National leagues. Their teams would crisscross the country, often playing in broken-down stadiums for little money. They would play the white teams in off-season exhibition games, where many white players recognized the talent of the black players. However, no one crossed the racial barrier until after World War II, when the first black players entered the major leagues. The Negro leagues gave a start to many of the great black baseball stars who emerged then, including Leroy "Satchel" Paige, Jackie Robinson, and Roy Campanella.

In the exciting 1934 World Series, the National League champion St. Louis Cardinals—called the "gas house gang"—charged to victory. The gang included manager–second baseman Frankie Frisch, third baseman "Pepper" Martin, outfielder "Ducky" Medwick, and the pitching brothers "Dizzy" and "Daffy" Dean. Each of the Deans won two games to win the Series for the Cardinals. One of baseball's greatest pitchers, Dizzy Dean won 120 games between 1932 and 1936. His career was cut short by an injury sustained in an All-Star Game.

The American League had the strikeout king of the era in Bob Feller, who made his major-league debut with the Cleveland Indians

1941: Baseball's Banner Year

By winning the 1941 World Series, the Yankees brought to a close one of baseball's greatest years—and ended an era in professional baseball history. The U.S. entry into the war was just a few weeks away, and professional baseball would struggle to survive during the war years. Strikeout king Bob Feller left the mound in early 1942 to serve as a gun-crew chief on the U.S.S. *Alabama.*

Many other major leaguers entered the armed forces, too. When these athletes returned to the diamond after the war, baseball took on a whole new face.

In 1941 the great Lou Gehrig died. This left Bill Dickey, a catcher, and Joe DiMaggio to carry on the "Yankee Class," that quiet, polished style of play that all three players represented. DiMaggio did his part. In 1941 he set a major-league record by batting safely in 56 consecutive games.

DiMaggio's rival as a great hitter in 1941—and for years to come—was Ted Williams of the Boston Red Sox. Quick-tempered, opinionated, and often at odds with team management, Williams was a sensational hitter, as he proved in 1941. Williams's average was over .400 on the last day of the season, a doubleheader. Offered the chance to sit out the games and keep his average, Williams refused. With six hits in eight at-bats, he ended the season at .406 and became the last major leaguer to achieve a .400 season average.

◄ Ted Williams was a fearsome left-handed hitter for more than two decades.

at age 17 in 1936. In his first season he struck out 17 batters in one game. When he retired in 1956, he had achieved 266 victories, pitched 3 no-hitters and 12 one-hitters, and struck out 18 batters in one game and 348 in a season. Known as "Rapid Robert," Feller's fastball was once clocked at 98.6 miles per hour.

The Yankees began to dominate baseball again in 1936, winning the World Series in 1936 through 1939 and in 1941 and 1943. Babe Ruth was traded in 1934 to play for the Boston Braves. He retired the following year at the age of 40. Even so, the Yankees had many stars—especially Lou Gehrig and DiMaggio. First baseman and batting ace Gehrig earned the nickname "The Iron Horse" because of his build, strength, and endurance. He played in a record 2,130 consecutive games between 1925 and 1939 and had a career total of 1,991 RBIs (third highest in history). In 1939 Gehrig was diagnosed with a fatal disease, a hardening of the spinal cord that became known as Lou Gehrig's disease. His touching farewell at Yankee Stadium left no one with dry eyes. In 1942, one year after Gehrig's death, Gary Cooper portrayed him in the movie of his life, *Pride of the Yankees.*

Gehrig's teammate, Joe DiMaggio, was another great hitter. Known as the "Yankee Clipper" because of his graceful style, DiMaggio is considered by many as the best all-around centerfielder of all time. During his 13 years as a Yankee, he helped the team win ten American League pennants and nine World Series.

Another standout hitter, Ted Williams, came to prominence in 1939 with the Boston Red Sox. During his career he captured six batting titles, played in 18 All-Star Games, and achieved a lifetime batting average of .344. Baseball historians wonder what more he could have done had he not spent five seasons in the armed forces. Indeed, the same could be said of many great ballplayers of this era, whose careers were reduced by the war.

Football

BOWL GAMES AND THE NFL

College football was more popular than the professional game during the 1930s. Pasadena's Rose Bowl had been a tradition since 1902, but other postseason bowls started in this era: the Sugar (in New Orleans, 1935), Sun (in El Paso, 1936), Orange (in Miami, 1937), and Cotton (in Dallas, 1937). The basic modern offense, the T-formation, emerged during the late 1930s and caused a sensation in 1940. The speed of the T-formation helped Stanford win all its games—as well as the Rose Bowl—that season. Notre Dame and Army dominated college football during the 1940s using the "T."

By 1933 the professional National Football League was split into the Eastern and Western divisions. The top team in each division met in a title game at the end of each season. The college football draft system was started in 1936, with the last-place team in the NFL

NEW HALL OF FAME INDUCTS FIRST FIVE BASEBALL GREATS

In the early 1930s, public interest in baseball began to decline. Then worried baseball executives seized upon a 1907 report that fixed the game's origins with Abner Doubleday at Cooperstown, New York, in 1839. The commissioner began to prepare an elaborate centennial celebration for 1939.

Plans for the celebration included creation of a Hall of Fame at Cooperstown. In 1936 the Baseball Writers Association of America elected the first five players to that Hall: Ty Cobb, Walter Johnson, Christy Mathewson, Babe Ruth, and Honus Wagner.

With much ballyhoo, the National Baseball Museum and Hall of Fame was dedicated on June 12, 1939. As the baseball leaders had hoped, the publicity helped to revive enthusiasm for the game.

The popular legend of Abner Doubleday's "invention" of baseball in 1839 is now known to be false. However, the appeal of the legend has not faded for the fans who visit Cooperstown.

BIRTHS . . .

Hank Aaron, baseball player,
    1934
A. J. Foyt, race-car driver, 1935
Wilt Chamberlain, basketball
    player, 1936
Jack Nicklaus, golfer, 1940
Muhammad Ali, boxer, 1942
Billie Jean King, tennis player,
    1943

. . . AND DEATHS

Knute Rockne, football coach,
    1931
James J. Corbett, boxer, 1933
Ray Ewry, track star, 1937
Howie Morenz, hockey player,
    1937
Lou Gehrig, baseball player, 1941
Kenesaw Mountain Landis,
    baseball commissioner, 1944

choosing first in the selection of graduating players.

The forward pass was used more frequently as an offensive strategy, thanks primarily to the first great passing quarterback, "Slingin'" Sammy Baugh of Texas Christian University (1934–1936). As quarterback for the Washington Redskins for 16 years, he won league titles in 1937 and 1942 and held all passing records when he retired. Another star player was Don Hutson, All-American at University of Alabama (1932–1934), whom some consider the best pass receiver in football history. As an end for the Green Bay Packers (1935–1945), he set an NFL record by catching passes in 95 consecutive games.

Olympics

OWENS VERSUS HITLER

The 1930s brought international acclaim to several American sports figures, especially in track and field. One of the most admired athletes was Glenn Cunningham, who overcame severe leg burns to set high school, collegiate, national, and world records for the mile. The most famous miler of the 1930s, Cunningham recorded his best indoor time—4 minutes, 4.4 seconds—in 1938.

At the 1932 summer Olympic Games in Los Angeles, American runner Edward Tolan won the 100- and 200-meter races to become the first black gold medalist. The sensation of the summer games was 18-year-old Mildred "Babe"

Didrikson, whose gold-medal performances set world records in the javelin throw (143 feet 4 inches) and 80-meter hurdles (11.7 seconds).

The star of the 1932 and 1936 winter Olympic Games was Norwegian-born figure skater Sonja Henie, who captured her second and third gold medals (her first had come in 1928). She also won ten consecutive world championships from 1927 to 1936. Americans turned out in record numbers to see her perform with her own skating company after she turned professional in 1936. The popularity of Henie's skating tours and the Hollywood movies featuring her spectacular talent boosted the sport of ice skating. Two Olympic swimming champions (Johnny Weissmuller and Buster Crabbe) starred in Hollywood as well.

One of the most notable athletes of the time was African-American track star Jesse Owens. On May 25, 1935, Owens had the best one-day performance in track and field history at the world championships. He equaled the world record in the 100-yard dash and set new records in the long jump, 220-yard dash, and 220-yard low hurdles. His long jump record (8.13 meters) stood for 25 years.

Owens's main feat came at the 1936 summer Olympics held in Berlin, where he was declared "Athlete of the Games." He won four gold medals—in the 100 meters, the 200 meters, the long jump, and the 4-by-100-meter relay. His stunning victories destroyed Hitler's scheme to make the games a showcase for Aryan supremacy.

Hitler and the Olympics

▲ Jesse Owens's performance at the Berlin Olympics won him the title "Athlete of the Games."

Adolf Hitler wanted to use the 1936 summer Olympic Games in Berlin to show the greatness of his Third Reich. He boasted that the games would demonstrate the superiority of the Aryan race through the victories of his German athletes. To achieve his goal, Hitler committed to the cause all the country's resources. He even used his propaganda machine to keep the world informed of all preparations.

Before the games began, some countries expressed uneasiness about Nazi racial policies and anti-Semitism, but Hitler promised the International Olympic Committee that he would accept their authority and observe all rules. A special envoy of the U.S. Olympic Committee met with Hitler to get his guarantee that there would be no discrimination against Jews or blacks, a condition of U.S. participation.

As the Olympic flame was brought into the stadium—carried from ancient Olympia in Greece for the first time in the history of the modern games—Hitler beamed in the glow of world acclaim. The modern facilities, detailed organization, precision timing, and lavish entertainments showcased Hitler's dynamic new Germany. To make sure the world knew everything that was happening, Hitler asked 3,000 media representatives to attend. He also had his personal filmmaker, Leni Riefenstahl, create a documentary of the games.

What Riefenstahl documented, however, was the complete failure of Hitler's racial theories. Although German athletes won the most medals, Americans dominated track and field events (winning 12 out of 23 gold medals) largely through the efforts of black athletes. Ten African-Americans won eight gold, three silver, and two bronze medals, negating Nazi propaganda that called them "black auxiliaries."

Hitler's racial "truths" took their heaviest blow from Jesse Owens, who captured four gold medals in track and field to become "Athlete of the Games." Owens became the most popular figure of the games, endearing himself to spectators with his cheerful, quiet manner and his amazing abilities. The final of the long jump, which pitted Owens against the German Lutz Long, stood out as the most exciting and politically charged competition. Each man had outjumped the other in six successive attempts when Owens finally made the winning jump.

Long was a better sportsman than his leader. After the meet, Hitler had to watch him and Owens walking together, Long's arm draped over Owens's shoulders in congratulations.

Jesse Owens's Records in Track and Field

Event	Year	Record
100-yd. dash	1935	9.4 sec.
Long jump	1935	26 ft. 8^1/$_4$ in.
220-yd. dash	1935	20.3 sec.
220-yd. hurdles	1935	22.6 sec.
100-m. run*	1936	10.3 sec.
200-m. run*	1936	20.7 sec.
Long jump*	1936	26 ft. 5^1/$_2$ in.

*Olympic record

LOUIS RULES THE ROOST

During the 1930s professional boxing set and followed high standards of conduct. From 1937 the sport was heavily promoted at many large arenas such as Madison Square Garden in New York City. Its popularity grew, however, largely due to the career of Joe Louis, world heavyweight champion from 1937 to 1948. Two other major boxers of the time were American Henry Armstrong and German Max Schmeling.

In 1938 Henry Armstrong became the only fighter ever to hold three world professional boxing championships—featherweight, welterweight, and lightweight—simultaneously. He was nicknamed "Perpetual Motion" because of his speed, stamina, and aggressive style.

German boxing champion Max Schmeling exemplified what Hitler had called the Aryan superman, especially when he defeated black American fighter Joe Louis in a 12-round decision in 1936. However, the German's superior image vanished in a rematch two years later. Louis knocked him out and sent him to the hospital in the first round of their rematch.

Louis, affectionately called "The Brown Bomber," rates as one of the greatest heavyweights in boxing history. After winning the Amateur Athletic Union light-heavyweight title in 1934, he turned professional. That same year he defeated 12 opponents, then destroyed 10 more by the late spring of 1935. Louis was famous for his smooth footwork, brutal left jab, and ability to deliver a knockout punch with either hand. He defeated James Braddock to become world heavyweight champion in 1937. He took on all challengers, defending his title a record 25 times during his 11 years as champion. That reign as champ was the longest in boxing history, and his lifetime professional record was 68 wins (54 by knockouts) and 3 losses.

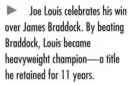

► Joe Louis celebrates his win over James Braddock. By beating Braddock, Louis became heavyweight champion—a title he retained for 11 years.

Tennis

NEW STARS NET POPULARITY

Attendance at amateur and professional tennis matches increased during the 1930s. One reason was the outstanding play of such champions as Donald Budge, Helen Hull Jacobs, and Helen Wills Moody.

One of the greatest tennis players of all time, Budge was famous for his powerful serve and for his backhand, which he used as an attacking stroke rather than as the usual defensive stroke. His consistency and all-court game helped the U.S. team win the Davis Cup—for the first time—in 1937. The following year Budge led the U.S. team that defended that title. In 1938 Budge demonstrated his dominance of the men's game. He became the first player to win the Grand Slam—the singles championships of Australia, France, Britain, and the United States.

Helen Hull Jacobs was known for her fine volley and her net play. She won Wimbledon in 1936 and was the U.S. women's singles champ from 1932 through 1935.

Her major rival was Helen Wills Moody, who won the Wimbledon women's singles a then-record eight times: 1927–1930, 1932–1933, 1935, and 1938. Moody was also a seven-time winner of the U.S. women's championship. Nicknamed the "Snow Queen" and "Little Miss Poker Face" because she showed no emotion during matches, Moody liked to play the back court and was known for her powerful, full-length drives.

Golf

THE SPREAD OF TOURNAMENTS

One of the important developments in golf during the Depression era was the replacement of hickory shafts with steel shafts on golf clubs. Another major change was organizational. In 1936 the Professional Golfers Association (PGA) hired a full-time tournament director, Fred Corcoran. Under Corcoran, the number of tournaments increased from 11 to 30, and the amount of prize money from a range of $3,000 to $10,000 to a total of $750,000 by 1946. The annual Masters Tournament was started in 1934.

Benefiting from these changes were two outstanding professional golfers—Gene Sarazen and Byron Nelson. Sarazen won the U.S. and British Opens in 1932, the PGA title in 1933, and the Masters in 1935. He also introduced the sand wedge into the game. One of the greatest players in golf history, "Lord" Nelson won the U.S. Open, the Masters, and two PGA championships between 1937 and 1942. He dominated the game during the war years, winning 19 tournaments (and 11 in a row) in 1945. He was named Athlete of the Year in 1944 and 1945.

Among women golfers, Glenna Collett (Vare) and Betty Jameson were standouts. Collett won the British Open in 1930 and the U.S. Women's Amateur Championship six times. Jameson won her first tournament in 1934 at age 15, then went on to win the USGA championship in 1939 and 1940.

NEW GAME MAKES GOLF AVAILABLE TO ALL

Miniature golf, invented in Chattanooga, Tennessee, in 1929, boomed during the Depression years. The game required only a putter on an obstacle-strewn nine-hole course. Its inventor, John Garnet Carter, patented the name "Tom Thumb" and sold franchise rights. It was truly a sport for the masses: it demanded neither wealth nor athletic ability.

Almost overnight, the landscape was dotted with miniature golf courses. By 1930, 40,000 courses nationwide employed over 200,000 people. New York City and Los Angeles each had a thousand courses.

Some courses were more elaborate and expensive, and courted upper-class players. At Covey's Cocoanut Grove in Salt Lake City, Utah, tuxedoed and gowned couples played miniature golf with caddies. This "exclusive" course cost 30 cents per round in the afternoon and 50 cents per round at night; caddies were 75 cents extra.

THE DRIVE-IN MAKES ITS DEBUT

The first drive-in movie theater opened in Camden, New Jersey, on June 6, 1933. Two shows were presented nightly on a 40- by 50-foot screen. The theater was built on 10 acres of land and could hold 500 cars at once.

"The Babe": Woman for All Sports

Considered by many to be America's greatest female athlete of all time, Mildred "Babe" Didrikson (1914–1956) excelled in basketball, golf, track and field, baseball, and swimming. Indeed, Didrikson participated in almost every sport—from billiards to boxing—at some time during her life.

Growing up in Texas, she could run, jump, box, and play football and baseball better than most boys her age. In 1932 she gained national recognition by winning eight of ten events, including the 80-meter hurdles, the shotput, the broad jump, and the javelin throw, in the Amateur Athletic Union's National Women's Track and Field championships. At age 18, she became the star of the 1932 summer Olympics. She won gold medals in the javelin throw and the 80-meter hurdles (setting world records in both) and a silver medal in the high jump.

After the 1932 Olympics Didrikson turned professional. She began her career as a basketball player for an insurance company team. She was named All-American in the sport from 1939 to 1941. In 1938 she mar-ried pro wrestler George Zaharias and two years later opened her spectacular career in professional golf. By 1950 she had won every available championship of women's golf at least once and in 1947 had become the first American to win the British women's championship. Her outgoing personality and casual, uninhibited manner made her extremely popular; thousands of fans flocked to see her play. Affectionately called "The Babe," Didrikson brought public acceptance of women's golf.

She was so admired as an all-around athlete that she once pitched an inning for the Brooklyn Dodgers in an exhibition game, striking out Joe DiMaggio. She often worked out with the football team of Southern Methodist University.

In 1953 Didrikson underwent cancer surgery; doctors told her she would never play golf again. To the delight and inspiration of the public, she responded by winning the 1954 U.S. Open by a record twelve strokes. She went on to win four other championships that year and two more in 1955 before her deteriorating condition forced her to stop playing. No other athlete—male or female—has been quite like "The Babe."

THE EFFECT OF THE WAR

Through the influence of radio broadcasts, many professional athletes became heroes and heroines to Americans young and old. Even persons who were not actual sports fans knew of Babe Ruth, Lou Gehrig, Babe Didrikson, Helen Moody, and the giant of them all—Joe Louis. These and other sports greats were people to be admired; all Americans felt close to them. Their names and exploits were a regular part of conversations. Discussing sports helped ease the pain of everyday life. During the war, many of these stars used their fame to help the war effort. Louis, for instance, fought exhibition bouts around the world to entertain the troops.

During the war years many regular sporting events and championships were canceled. Professional baseball received permission from President Roosevelt to continue its games, but the quality of play fell sharply. With so many great players—like Feller, DiMaggio, and Williams—serving in the armed forces, baseball teams employed those under or over draft age, or otherwise ineligible for military service. Games were filled with confusion and disorder as many mediocre players built up terrible records. The situation was so bad that by the start of the 1945 World Series sportswriter Warren Brown was forced to observe, "I don't believe either team can win."

Many colleges dropped football, while the professional teams struggled to survive. At one point, the National Football League had to combine what was left of the Pittsburgh Steelers and the Philadelphia Eagles into one team that was called the Steagles. There were not enough players for two teams.

Tennis continued with a limited number of matches. However, no Olympic Games were held in 1940 or 1944. The USGA suspended all its golf events from 1942 to 1945, although other tournaments were still held. Before Britain halted all golf events during the height of the war, a new wartime rule was adopted. The rule acknowledged the unusual conditions brought on by the war: "A player whose stroke is affected by the simultaneous explosion of a bomb or shell . . . may play another ball from the same place. Penalty, one stroke."

Leisure

AMERICA AT REST

Although most Americans struggled through the Depression, they still had a number of opportunities to relax and escape from reality. Two World's Fairs gave millions a view of the past and the future. Magazines like *Vogue, Esquire,* and the new photojournal *Life* kept people up-to-date on the activities of society glamour girls and popular entertainers.

High Society
A new cafe society formed during the 1930s. It gathered in fashionable members of high society, entertainers, gossip columnists, and European nobility who came from

BINGO!

The Great Depression forced most Americans to devise inexpensive forms of entertainment. Parlor games, jigsaw puzzles, and card games such as contract bridge all enjoyed huge popularity during the 1930s. One game that offered socializing and the chance to win money was public bingo, first played in churches in 1935.

Although some people criticized bingo as a legal form of gambling, the game was very popular. The hope of striking it rich in a single evening appealed to many, as did the opportunity to meet other enthusiasts. Bingo declined somewhat in popularity during World War II, but it has never disappeared.

TRAILERS HIT THE ROAD

With improvements in the highway system, Americans were increasingly lured by the romance of the open road and their country's scenic wonders. After investing in a trailer that could be hitched to an automobile, a family could set out on a relatively inexpensive camping vacation.

By 1936 the age of the trailer reached full swing. By that time there were an estimated 160,000 trailers on the roadways. Observers on January 1, 1937, counted an average of 25 trailers per hour crossing the state line into Florida. Some statisticians predicted that soon one-half of the population would be living in trailers.

the war-torn continent to live in America. These carefree, publicity-hungry people were constantly photographed at places like New York City's Stork Club, "21," El Morocco, and the Colony—which used to be speakeasies during the Prohibition era.

Glamour girl Brenda Frazier made headlines dancing until dawn with the movie star Douglas Fairbanks Jr. and created a new fashion when she wore a strapless evening gown. Her male counterpart was the dashing, handsome, and wealthy man-about-town Alfred G. Vanderbilt, who was chosen best-dressed man in the country. However, at the center of cafe society was an ordinary-looking woman from Iowa named Elsa Maxwell. "Everyone who was anyone" attended her lavish parties, at which she was queen.

Some publications attacked these wealthy socialites. They published critical pictures or stories protesting the luxury of high society in the midst of the Depression.

The World's Fairs

The Chicago World's Fair (1933–1934) attracted about 100 million people even though it was held during the worst years of the Depression. Optimistically called the "Century of Progress Exposition," the fair featured an eight-acre Hall of Science showing the progress of civilization since the founding of Chicago in 1833.

New York staged an elaborate World's Fair in 1939 and 1940, as the Depression was finally winding down. People could at last look hopefully to "The World of Tomorrow," as the fair was called. It covered over 1,200 acres and was the biggest and costliest international exposition yet held. There were 65 miles of paved streets and footpaths. Three hundred futuristic buildings housed 1,500 exhibitors from 33 states, 58 foreign countries, and 1,300 businesses. The fair featured such exhibits as television and a talking robot named Elektro. General Electric's scientific display demonstrated human-

▶ The sundial (center) and statue of George Washington beyond it welcomed visitors to New York's World's Fair. Other buildings stretched in all directions.

made lightning and synthetic thunder. In General Motors' popular "Futurama" exhibit, people sat in chairs on a conveyor belt and rode the "highway of tomorrow" over a huge scale model of what America would look like in 1960.

Fashion Trends

The 1930s brought a return to a more feminine and romantic look in women's fashions. Blonde hair and clothing emphasizing the female form made the ideal look, influenced by film stars Mae West and Jean Harlow. By 1936 the straight skirt, called a pencil skirt, became the rage, and slacks for women gained popularity. The backless one-piece bathing suit with shoulder straps was introduced when sunbathing became popular. Footwear was varied—from platform shoes and wedged heels to thick high heels with ankle straps. Clothing for sports received special attention.

The war years dramatically changed the fashion industry in America, which was cut off from fashion trends usually influenced by French designers. Furthermore, government regulation limited the amount of fabric that civilian manufacturers could use. As a result, coats had no cuffs, blouses had no pockets or ruffles, and skirts were skimpier.

Americans cleverly created some new fashions during these hard times. The wraparound skirt, for instance, made up for the wartime ban on zippers and metal fasteners for commercial use. To replace stockings, which were unavailable, women painted their legs with makeup and used an eyebrow pen-

cil to draw seams. Fashion also took ideas from military uniforms. Army corps hats, gowns with eagle-wing decorations, and the famous Eisenhower jacket all became popular items of apparel.

The Teenage Market

By the 1940s the American adolescent had emerged as a clearly defined personality—the teenager. The 1920s had started this change, which the war intensified. Since men over age 18 were away fighting, younger boys suddenly had jobs, money, and clout. Adolescent girls had money, too, from babysitting for women who worked night shifts at factories. These teenagers wanted to spend their money, and manufacturers were quick to respond. *Seventeen* magazine appeared in 1944, and the clothing and record industries focused more attention on teenage trends. Teenagers would become an even more important segment of the population—and the marketplace—after the war.

▲ This 1939 photograph shows jitterbuggers dancing to the music of Artie Shaw's band. The dancers were competing for the title of year's best couple in Los Angeles.

SIR MALCOLM CAMPBELL SETS SPEED RECORDS

Malcolm Campbell first achieved fame for his speed records in cars. In 1927 he established his first land speed record—174.22 miles per hour. On September 3, 1935, he became the first driver ever to reach over 300 miles per hour on land.

His passion for boat racing led him to design a hydroplane (called *Bluebird* like his car). In 1937 Campbell set a new water speed record of 129.42 miles per hour. That year he held the world's speed records for land *and* water. In 1939 he beat his old water record in the *Bluebird II* with a speed of 141.74 miles per hour.

"*O*h, the humanity!"

—Herb Morrison, on the explosion
of the airship *Hindenburg*, 1937

**G*ood evening,
Mr. and Mrs.
America, and all
the ships at sea.***

—Walter Winchell, 1932

A dust storm hit,
And it hit like thunder;
It dusted us over,
And it covered us under;

Blocked out the traffic
And blocked out the sun.
Straight for home
All the people did run.

—Woody Guthrie,
"So Long, It's Been Good to Know Yuh
(Dusty Old Dust)," 1936

...Now, nearer home, comes a special announcement from Trenton, New Jersey. It is reported that at 8:50 P.M. a huge, flaming object, believed to be a meteorite, fell on a farm in the neighborhood of Grovers Mill, New Jersey, 22 miles from Trenton. The flash in the sky was visible within a radius of several hundred miles and the noise of the impact was heard as far north as Elizabeth....

—From "The War of the Worlds," a radio play
based on the novel by H. G. Wells,
broadcast October 30, 1938,
by Orson Welles and the Mercury Theatre

RAISE GIANT FROGS

START IN YOUR BACKYARD—
BREEDER LAYS
10,000 EGGS YEARLY

Men and Women! Get into this interesting new industry *now!* Make a frog pond *in your backyard* and expand with increase.

—American Frog Canning Company ad,
1936

BEGGING IS UNNECESSARY

The City Provides for Its Destitute and Homeless

—Sign in New York subways, 1930s

"*W*hen they need us they call us migrants. When we've picked their crops we're bums and we've got to get out."

—A migrant worker

W*ho knows what evil lurks in the hearts of men? The Shadow knows!*

—"The Shadow," 1936

VOICES OF THE ERA

"*A*merica hasn't been as happy in three years as they are today, no money, no banks, no work, no nothing, but they know they got a man in there who is wise to Congress, wise to our so-called big men. The whole country is with him, just so he does something. If he burned down the capitol, we would cheer and say 'Well, we at least got a fire started anyhow.'"

—Will Rogers, 1933

Who's that little chatterbox? The one with the pretty auburn locks? Who can it be? It's "Little Orphan Annie."

—"Little Orphan Annie" theme, 1931

"*L*ook at me. Worked myself up from nothing to a state of extreme poverty."

—From the Marx Brothers film *Monkey Business,* 1931

Benny: Now look here, Allen, I don't care what you say about my singing on your *own* program, but after all, *I've* got listeners!

Allen: Keep your family out of this.

Benny: Well, my family likes my singing . . . and my violin playing, too.

Allen: Your violin playing! Why, I just heard that a horse committed suicide when he found out your violin bow was made from his tail. . . .

—Excerpt from "Jell-O Program," starring Jack Benny, with guest Fred Allen

There's a new killer diller
There's a new Harlem thriller
A new way to ruin the rugs
A new dance for Jitter Bugs.

The Flat Foot Floogee with the Floy Floy
The Flat Foot Floogee with the Floy Floy
The Flat Foot Floogee with the Floy Floy
Floy Doy, Floy Doy, Floy Doy, Floy Doy;

The Flat Foot Floogee with the Flou Flou
The Flat Foot Floogee with the Flou Flou
The Flat Foot Floogee with the Flou Flou,
Flou Dow, Flou Dow, Flou Dow, Flou Dow.

—Slim Gaillard, Slam Stewart, and Bud Green, "The Flat Foot Floogee," 1938

"*F*rankly, my dear, I don't give a damn."

—Clark Gable to Vivien Leigh in the film *Gone with the Wind,* 1939

And it came about that the owners no longer worked on their farms. They farmed on paper, and they forgot the land, the smell, the feel of it, and remembered only that they owned it, remembered only what they gained and lost by it. And some of the farms grew so large that one man could not even conceive of them any more, so large that it took batteries of bookkeepers to keep track of interest and gain and loss; chemists to test the soil, to replenish; straw bosses to see that the stooping men were moving along the rows as swiftly as the material of their bodies could stand. Then such a farmer really became a storekeeper, and kept a store. He paid the men, and sold them food, and took the money back. And after a while he did not pay the men at all, and saved bookkeeping. These farms gave food on credit. A man might work and feed himself; and when the work was done, he might find that he owed money to the company. And the owners not only did not work the farms any more, many of them had never seen the farms they owned.

—John Steinbeck, *The Grapes of Wrath,* 1939

CHURCHILL PLEDGES WAR TILL EMPIRE ENDS

—*New York Times,*
June 5, 1940

PRESIDENT ROOSEVELT IS DEAD; TRUMAN SWORN IN AS SUCCESSOR

—*New York Herald Tribune, April 13, 1945*

"*You begin to feel that you can't go on forever without being hurt. I feel that I have used up all my chances. And I hate it. I don't want to be killed.*"

—*Ernie Pyle, 1945*

"*All they forfeit is their freedom.*"

—*Time,* referring to
Japanese-Americans
sent to internment
camps, 1941

SMITH AND BAGBY STOP YANKEE STAR

DiMaggio, Up for Last Time in Eighth,
Hits into a Double Play with Bases Full

—*July 16, 1941*

As one
of the Japanese
I gather my belongings.

—*Keiho, imprisoned issei,*
World War II

You are about to embark upon the Great Crusade, toward which we have striven these many months. The eyes of the world are upon you. The hopes and prayers of liberty-loving people everywhere march with you. In company with our brave Allies and brothers-in-arms on other Fronts, you will bring about the destruction of the German war machine, the elimination of Nazi tyranny over the oppressed peoples of Europe, and security for ourselves in a free world.

—*General Dwight D. Eisenhower,*
excerpt from a message
to Allied forces,
June 5, 1944

HESS, DESERTING HITLER, FLIES TO SCOTLAND; BERLIN REPORTED HIM MISSING AND INSANE

—*New York Times, May 13, 1941*

Victory won't wait for the nation that's late.

—*Big Ben Clocks ad,*
1942

Won't you try Wheaties?
They're whole wheat with all of the bran.
Won't you try Wheaties?
For wheat is the best food of man.

—*From "The Wheaties Song," 1939*

VOICES OF THE ERA

With his faithful Indian companion, Tonto, the daring and resourceful masked rider of the plains led the fight for law and order, in the early western United States. Nowhere in the pages of history can one find a greater champion of justice. Return with us now to those thrilling days of yesteryear. . . . From out of the past come the thundering hoofbeats of the great horse Silver! The Lone Ranger rides again!

—"The Lone Ranger," 1942

"I cannot forecast to you the action of Russia. It is a riddle wrapped in a mystery inside an enigma."

—Sir Winston Spencer Churchill, 1939

Wear it up, wear it out, make it do, or do without.

—Home front saying, 1943

"Of all the gin joints in all the towns in all the world, she walks into mine."

—Humphrey Bogart in the film *Casablanca*, 1942

Katherine:	What's Rosebud?
Raymond:	That's what he said when he died. . . .
Louise:	If you could have found out what Rosebud meant, I bet that would've explained everything.
Thompson:	No, I don't think so. No. Mr. Kane was a man who got everything he wanted, and then lost it. Maybe Rosebud was something he couldn't get or something he lost. Anyway, it wouldn't have explained anything. I don't think any word can explain a man's life. No, I guess Rosebud is just a piece in a jigsaw puzzle, a missing piece.

—From the film *Citizen Kane*, 1941

Praise the Lord, and pass the ammunition And we'll all stay free!

—"Praise the Lord and Pass the Ammunition," by Frank Loesser, 1942

"I have nothing to offer but blood, toil, tears and sweat."

—Sir Winston Spencer Churchill, 1940

Glossary

Allies: during World War II, the countries that fought against Germany, Italy, and Japan, including the United Kingdom, the USSR, and the United States

annex: to incorporate new territory into an existing state or country

antibiotic: a drug that fights and destroys bacterial infections and is widely used to treat and prevent diseases

anti-Semitic: hostile toward Jewish people and their culture

Axis: during World War II, the countries (including Germany, Japan, and Italy) that fought against the Allies

bureaucracy: administration, usually of a government, marked by the employment of nonelected officials, excessive hierarchies, and red tape

capitalism: an economic system controlled by individuals and corporations rather than by government, characterized by open competition in a free market

collective bargaining: negotiations between union representatives and an employer to determine wages, hours, benefits, and working conditions

collective farm: a farm or group of farms organized and worked by a group of laborers under government supervision

deportation: the removal of a person whose presence in a country is illegal or undesirable

fascism: a government system in which an extreme right-wing dictatorship controls a nation

genocide: the deliberate extermination of a race

ghetto: a poor section of a city occupied by a specific racial or ethnic group

hybrid: the offspring of two plants or animals of different species or varieties

inaugural: relating to the ceremonial induction of a person into office

inflation: a general increase in prices and fall in the purchasing value of money in an economy

intervention: the act of interfering, usually by force or threat of force, in the affairs of a nation

isolationism: a national policy of avoiding conflicts and alliances with other nations

nationalism: loyalty and devotion to a nation

nationalize: to transfer ownership of land and property from private owners to the government

nuclear fission: the splitting of the nucleus of atoms, resulting in the release of large amounts of energy

nutrient: a nourishing substance

private enterprise: businesses owned and managed by individuals or corporations rather than by a government

propaganda: government-created publicity intended to spread information and ideas that influence people's opinions

purge: to rid a nation, political party, or other group of persons who are considered undesirable

rationing: supplying fixed amounts of food to military personnel or citizens during times of scarcity

recession: a temporary decline in economic activity

social welfare program: a program established to help specific groups, such as the elderly or the unemployed

speculation: the act of taking financial risks in the hope of making a large profit

subsidy: a grant or gift of money

tariff: a charge imposed by a government on imports and exports

totalitarian: of or relating to a form of government in which one individual or party is in complete control

unconstitutional: not in accordance with a particular constitution

welfare state: a social system in which the state assumes responsibility for the social welfare of its citizens

Suggested Readings

General

Abbott, Carl. *Urban America in the Modern Age, 1920 to Present.* H. Davidson, 1987.

Allen, Frederick Lewis. *The Big Change, 1900–1950.* Bantam, 1965.

Blum, Daniel. *A Pictorial History of the Silent Screen.* Grosset & Dunlap, 1953.

Cairns, Trevor. *The Twentieth Century.* Cambridge University Press, 1984.

Cantor, Norman F., and Michael S. Werthman, eds. *The History of Popular Culture.* Macmillan, 1968.

Churchill, Allen. *The Great White Way.* E. P. Dutton, 1962.

Daniels, Roger. *Coming to America: A History of Immigration and Ethnicity in American Life.* HarperCollins, 1990.

Davids, Jules. *America and the World of Our Time.* Random House, 1960.

Ewing, Elizabeth. *History of Twentieth Century Fashion.* Barnes & Noble, 1986.

Filene, Peter G. *Him/Her/Self: Sex Roles in Modern America.* Johns Hopkins University Press, 1986.

Flink, James J. *The Automobile Age.* MIT, 1988.

Freidel, Frank. *America in the Twentieth Century.* Knopf, 1960.

Goff, Richard. *The Twentieth Century: A Brief Global History.* John Wiley, 1983.

Hine, Darlene Clark, ed. *Black Women in American History.* Carlson Publishing, 1990.

Manchester, William. *The Glory and the Dream: A Narrative History of America, 1932–1972.* Little, Brown, 1974.

May, George S., ed. *The Automobile Industry, 1920–1980.* Facts on File, 1989.

Morgan, Robert P. *Twentieth-Century Music: A History of Musical Style in Modern Europe and America.* Norton, 1991.

Noble, David W., David A. Horowitz, and Peter N. Carroll. *Twentieth Century Limited: A History of Recent America.* Houghton Mifflin, 1980.

Norman, Philip. *The Road Goes On Forever: Portraits from a Journey Through Contemporary Music.* Simon & Schuster, 1982.

Olderman, Murray. *Nelson's Twentieth Century Encyclopedia of Baseball.* Nelson, 1963.

Oliver, John W. *History of American Technology.* Books on Demand UMI, 1956.

Ritter, Lawrence S. *The Story of Baseball.* Morrow, 1983.

Sklar, Robert. *Movie-Made America: A Cultural History of American Movies.* Random House, 1976.

Spaeth, Sigmund. *A History of Popular Music in America.* Random House, 1948.

Susman, Warren I. *Culture as History: The Transformation of American Society in the Twentieth Century.* Pantheon, 1984.

Taft, Philip. *Organized Labor in American History.* Harper & Row, 1964.

Vecsey, George, ed. *The Way It Was: Great Sports Events from the Past.* McGraw-Hill, 1974.

Zinn, Howard. *The Twentieth Century: A People's History.* Harper & Row, 1984.

About the Era

Agee, James, and Walker Evans. *Let Us Now Praise Famous Men.* Ballantine, 1974.

Barley, Ronald H. *The Home Front: U.S.A.* Time-Life, 1977.

Barry, James P. *Berlin Olympics, Nineteen Thirty-Six: Black American Athletes Counter Nazi Propaganda.* Franklin Watts, 1975.

Baxter, John. *Hollywood in the Thirties.* Barnes, 1968.

Bernstein, Irving. *A Caring Society: The New Deal, the Worker, and the Great Depression: A History of the American Worker, 1933–1941.* Houghton Mifflin, 1985.

Buchanan, A. Russell. *Black Americans in World War II.* Regina, 1977.

Daniels, Jonathan. *The Time Between the Wars.* Doubleday, 1966.

Frank, Anne. *The Diary of a Young Girl.* Doubleday, 1967.

Goldston, Robert. *The Great Depression: The United States in the Thirties.* Fawcett, 1978.

———. *The Road Between the Wars: 1918–1941.* Dial, 1978.

Hartmann, Susan M. *The Home Front and Beyond: American Women in the 1940s.* Twayne, 1982.

Keller, Mollie. *Winston Churchill.* Franklin Watts, 1984.

Leckie, Robert. *The Story of World War II.* Random House, 1964.

Lord, Walter. *Day of Infamy.* Holt, Rinehart and Winston, 1991.

Morgan, Ted. *FDR: A Biography.* Simon & Schuster, 1985.

Perrett, Geoffrey. *Days of Sadness, Years of Triumph: The American People, 1939–1945.* University of Wisconsin Press, 1985.

Sherwin, Martin J. *A World Destroyed: The Atomic Bomb and the Grand Alliance.* Random House, 1977.

Shirer, William L. *The Rise and Fall of the Third Reich: A History of Nazi Germany.* Simon & Schuster, 1960.

Snyder, Louis L. *World War II.* Franklin Watts, 1981.

Terkel, Studs. *Hard Times.* Avon, 1970.

———. *"The Good War": An Oral History of World War Two.* Pantheon, 1984.

Toland, John. *Adolf Hitler.* Doubleday, 1976.

———. *Infamy: Pearl Harbor and Its Aftermath.* Berkley Books, 1983.

Vatter, Harold. *The U.S. Economy in World War II.* Columbia University Press, 1985.

Ware, Susan. *Holding Their Own: American Women in the 1930s.* G. K. Hall, 1983.

Wilson, Edmund. *The Forties: From Notebooks and Diaries of the Period.* Farrar, Straus and Giroux, 1983.

Index

Note: A page number in italic indicates a table, map, graph, or illustration.